Bullying and Stress in the Workplace: Employers and Employees – A Guide

To my parents and family

Bullying and Stress in the Workplace: Employers and Employees – A Guide

John Eardly, B.L.

FOREWORD BY

RODERICK HORAN, BL

Published in 2002 by
First Law Limited
Merchant's Court,
Merchants Quay,
Dublin 8,
Ireland.

Typeset by Gough Typsetting Services, Dublin.

ISBN 1-904480-00-4

A catalogue record for this book
is available from the British Library.

Printed by Johnswood Press Ltd, Dublin.

Foreword

In approaching his subject, John Eardly has comprehensively identified the nature of the duties imposed on an employer in the employment relationship while he has also examined the jurisprudence establishing the principle that an employer must have regard for his employee's psychiatric health. This is frontier territory which has scarcely been charted or indeed explored in this country and it is true to say that the very notion of compensating an employee for a nervous disorder occasioned by his employer is a fraught one. In this regard, employers tend to react badly to allegations that they have bullied their employee or caused him to suffer a nervous breakdown. Again, there is an understandable scepticism which is not confined to the judiciary on the vexed subject of awarding damages for psychiatric illness and the English Law Commission in their *Consultation Paper on Liability for Psychiatric Illness* (LCCP No 137, 1995) commented at paragraph 1.9:

> "They argue that such illness can easily be faked; that, in any event, those who are suffering should be able to 'pull themselves together'; and that, even if they cannot do so, there is no good reason why defendants and, through them, those who pay insurance premiums should pay for their inability to do so."

This problem was pithily described in *Sutherland v. Hatton* [2002] I.R.L.R. 263, 269, paragraph 23 by Lady Justice Wale in the following terms:

> "Shylock could not say of a mental disorder 'If you prick us do we not bleed?' "

In one sense John Eardly's excellent text is prophetic in that absent equality legislation (which he considers and analyses) there are difficulties in classification if one seeks to identify the sources of the law of bullying/oppression in the workplace. This is clear from the title of his second Chapter which is headed **THE FINAL FRONTIER OF EMPLOYER LIABILITY?,** since an employee who is contending that he is the victim of stress at the hands of his employer is likely to invoke disparate and somewhat obscure torts including Intimidation, Conspiracy and the Reckless Infliction of Emotional Suffering.

Such an approach derives from the notion that the employer deliberately set about the harassment complained of although pleas will still be advanced in Negligence and Contract. There is doubtless an apprehension amongst practitioners that despite the tropical effulgence of the tort of Negligence in recent decades and a perception that it is user friendly, there are complex conceptual problems in Negligence relating to remoteness since the test for liability for the infliction of nervous shock, for example, still appears to be circumscribed by foreseeability.

This also explains why the plaintiff in *Walker v. Northumberland County Council* [1995] All E.R. 737, only succeeded in respect of his second nervous breakdown since the trial judge regarded the first break down as unforeseeable. This case is dealt with in detail by John Eardly and is clearly a seminal decision in that it specifically acknowledges that the employee who is the victim of psychiatric damage, can formulate his claim both in Contract and Negligence. This too is significant since it is not so very long ago that a servant could be directed by a Justice of the Peace in this country to return to his employer on pain of a sentence of hard labour and corporal punishment in default. Such a regimen (as provided for under the Servants' Act 1715) had less to do with notions of contract than status or servitude. However, the fragmentation of the old order has been reflected by a panoply of protective legislation and a significant alteration in judicial attitudes. Thus in *Woods v. W M Car Service (Peterborough) Limited* [1982] I.C.R. 693, Lord Denning M.R. commented that:

> "It is the duty of the employer to be good and considerate to his servants. Sometimes it is formulated as an implied term not to do anything likely to destroy the relationship of confidence between them..."

Ironically the clock in one sense has turned full circle in that the enactment of the Unfair Dismissal Act in 1977 provided that an employee could secure specific performance of his service contract although this remedy was confined to a Master under the Act of 1715.

On reading John Eardly's book, I was immediately struck by his clarity of exposition and the nature of his analyses particularly when he examines the difficult areas of risk assessment, training instruction, prevention and vicarious liability. And while this publication is not directed exclusively at the legal profession, I believe that it should be required reading for personnel managers and trade union officials alike. This view is reinforced by the abundance of the practical advice to be found on almost every page while the author is at pains to justify his conclusions by constant references to the very latest authorities. This is perhaps exemplified by his detailed parsing of the Court of Appeal judgments in England in *Sutherland v. Hatton* and three associated Appeals which were heard in tandem by the English Court of Appeal and are now reported in [2002] I.R.L.R. 263. The Lord Justices in these four cases pronounced, *inter alia*, that there are no specific restrictions applicable to claims by employees in respect of psychiatric illness or injury in that the ordinary principles of employer's liability apply. If this approach recommends itself to the Irish judiciary, (as I respectfully believe it might) then John Eardly's final frontier will have been reached since these judgments provide a comprehensive navigational aid for litigants and employers and their respective advisers.

Roddy Horan
October 2002

Preface

The theme of this book concerns the area of stress, bullying and harassment at work. Up until just a decade ago, it would have been difficult to imagine the extent to which the law has travelled along its current path of expanding the protection accorded to workers from these hazards in the course of their employment. Indeed, what many will find striking about this book is how very recent this area of law actually is. Therefore, the primary design of the author has been to give practical and accessible guidance on this rapidly expanding area of employment law. In doing so, all the relevant subjects are explained, distilled and brought together into one source. As such, I wish to extend my utmost gratitude to Mr Bart Daly of First Law, to BCM Hanby Wallace Solicitors, Dublin, to Mr Roderick Horan BL and to Gabriel Gavigan BL.

In particular, most employers have become familiar with and accustomed to their obligations to protect the health and safety of their employees at work. These obligations are derived from a number of diverse legal and professional sources and affect the employment relationship in a variety of ways. However, health and safety obligations, in the past, mainly touched upon the physical well being only of employees. This meant that mental health, when it was protected by the law at all, as in the case of nervous shock, was a more limited and secondary consideration to physical safety.

However, in recent years, this has all changed and changed utterly. Psychiatric and mental health and safety are now integral to the legal protection afforded to an employee in the workplace and indeed beyond it. Moreover, this form of protection is now completely independent of physical healthcare and is now valued as an important element, in itself, of an employer's duty of care. The issues of stress, bullying and harassment at work are the logical and most important examples of this development. Indeed, we are only at the very start of some even greater developments of this kind into the future. Therefore, practical guidance is also given here on the future trends that are likely to emerge over the coming years by analogy with both the ever-increasing body of new Irish decisions and with the development of the law and practices in the United Kingdom. These are also explained in detail.

Finally, as will be seen, understanding stress, bullying and harassment involves not only looking at the problem from the perspective of the civil courts which deal with personal injuries and the wrongful dismissal of employees but also from the perspective of the industrial relations tribunals and health and safety practices. In the latter cases, the new legislation, statutory Codes of Practice of 2002 and other health and safety reports and recommendations are relevant and are discussed also. Moreover, instances of bullying and harassment may now be penalised as actionable wrongs in themselves quite apart from the infliction of any personal injury or dismissal. This book draws together these different and often disjointed strands of law and practice in order to provide a clear and concise explanation to employers of their rights and obligations, how to meet them and the consequences of failure. As a result, employers, employees and their advisers must now equally familiarise themselves with what work-related stress, bullying and harassment mean for them and how to avoid the practical problems to which give rise.

As will be seen, the consequences of failure can be both serious and costly.

John Eardly
Law Library,
Four Court, Dublin 7.
14 October 2002

Table of Contents

Table of Cases

Ireland

England

Table of Legislation

Ireland

STATUTORY INSTRUMENTS

England

United States of America

CHAPTER 1

General Overview

> "The labour of a human being is not a commodity or article of commerce..."[1]

FROM SLAVERY TO SALARY: UNDERSTANDING EMPLOYMENT LAW

Throughout most of history, the regulation and control of labour has proved to be one of the darkest and most controversial episodes of our legal heritage. In particular, the law, in deference to its feudal roots and ties, traditionally enforced the entitlement of a master to his servant's labour as an obligation of ownership. It was upon this philosophy and social order that notions such as slavery and enforced or 'tied' servitude relied. However, as such notions were slowly eradicated, the law began to distinguish between the human being and the labour of that human being. Whereas, never again could a human being be owned, his labour, nevertheless, would remain a commodity in which, as a free individual, he was entitled to trade. The same principles of contract, developed in other areas of commerce, would henceforth be brought to bear onto the area of employment.

This new philosophy was driven as much by the *laisse-faire* ideals of the expanding capitalist economies of the Industrial Revolution and their need for a cheap and mobile labour force as by the growing importance and recognition afforded to the democratic ideals of universal human rights and freedoms. It meant that labour could be bought and sold

---

1 Article 6 of the Clayton Anti-Trust Act, United States.

and subjected to the very same processes of commercial bargaining and agreement into which the courts were always very reluctant to intervene.

However, from the middle of 19th Century onwards, it was ultimately recognised that this was not necessarily an entirely suitable principle for the relationship between parties to an employment contract, given the importance of the commodity itself to a person's existence and well-being. Also, by definition, unless there was an extreme labour shortage, the master always had greater commercial bargaining power than any potential servant and could thereby arbitrarily impose unfair and harsh conditions of employment upon him. Therefore, it became necessary to intervene in these private employment agreements to the extent necessary to ensure basic fairness and prevent undue exploitation.

The labour of a human being indeed was not to be a mere commodity or article of commerce. As such, this was the small but fundamental step in that long journey which brings us to where we find ourselves today.

The Sources of Law: A Brief Explanation

The primary sources of employment law applied are essentially fourfold.

> Firstly, there is the **Common Law**. This is judge-made law and has developed over generations of court decisions.
>
> Secondly, there is the **Legislation** and **Statutes** passed by the Oireachtas.
>
> Thirdly, the terms of a **Contract of Employment** may be important.

Finally, there is the **Constitution of Ireland**. This guarantees the fundamental rights of individuals. Any actions of an employer that have an impact on these fundamental rights must be carried out strictly in accordance with constitutional and natural justice.

The Remedies Available: Not quite a Minefield!

Finding your compass bearings

Employment law, as it is commonly understood, is not a uniform code of rules but, rather, an amalgamation of a number of different areas of law that impinge upon the relationship between an employer and an employee. These different areas of law will become clear in the course of this handbook. However, by way of brief summary, employers must familiarise themselves with the following basic concepts and definitions. Essentially, the three most important courses of action employees adopt are as follows.

1. Court proceedings seeking civil damages for personal injuries sustained in the course of employment

Such a claim will normally include the following allegations:

Negligence;

Breach of Contract;

Breach of Statute

Negligence

If an employee is alleging that he or she has suffered a

personal injury in the course of his employment, then he or she is primarily alleging the occurrence of a civil wrong or '*tort*' known as **negligence**. This is a common law relief and must be pursued through the civil courts.

Duty of Care

A tort arises out of a **duty of care** that one person owes another because of the nature of the relationship between them. A claim that a person failed to discharge that duty grounds the allegation of **negligence** against him or her. **The relationship between an employer and his employees is one in which a duty of care is owed**. At common law, six specific duties owed by an employer to his employees have been identified in Ireland:

- The employer will provide an employee with a safe system of work;
- The employer will provide an employee with a safe place of work;
- The employer will provide safe plant and machinery;
- The employer will engage competent employees and a safe number thereof;
- The duty to promulgate and enforce rules of conduct for employees that would make work safe;
- The duty to give warning of dangers of which the employee might reasonably be expected to remain in ignorance.[2]

---

[2] *Browne v. Ventelo Telecommunications (Ireland) Limited,* Employment Appeals Tribunal, Dublin, UD 597/2001, July 16, 2002.

Reasonableness

Whether an employer is ultimately found to be negligent will be measured on a number of grounds by the **legal standard** applied by the courts. What the standard is in any given situation will depend on what is 'reasonable' in all the circumstances of the case.

Damage

In these cases, can the employee show an injury or material damage sustained? If so, the remedy granted is that of **Damages**. In terms of occupational injury actions, damages are amounts of monetary compensation that seek to place the plaintiff in the position he would have been had he not suffered the injury. They are divided between special and general damages.

Special Damages refer to the liquidated or calculable loss that a plaintiff has already suffered as a result of his injury, namely, medical treatment, loss of earnings to date, expenses etc.

General Damages are a non-liquidated amount relating to the trauma and suffering brought upon a person as a result of the injury or damage alleged. They may also relate to any future loss of earnings that the employee may incur. In calculating such an amount, the courts will have regard to their earlier judicial decisions and precedents dealing with similar instances and similar types of accident in the past.

Therefore, the amount of possible financial exposure an employer may face is one of the matters on which he or she *should always* seek the advice of his or her lawyers as in many cases it will come down to the facts of a particular case.

Breach of contract

As part of the same personal injury claim for damages, an employee may also allege a **breach of his employment contract**, as well as the tort of negligence. The difference between the two is that, in a claim for negligence, the claim arises out of the specific relationship between the parties creating the legal duty of care whereas, in a breach of contract claim, the claim arises out of the agreed terms of a contract between the parties, whether expressed in writing between the parties or implied by the court.

Implied terms

An implied term is one that, although not expressly included in the written contract, is so important to the nature of the relationship between an employer and an employee that the law requires it to be a term of every such agreement and includes it as such. Therefore, at common law, where a contract fails to expressly provide otherwise, it will be implied that the employer agrees to take reasonable steps to protect the safety, health or welfare of his employees in the workplace. As such, the failure to do so is a breach of contract.

Breach of statute

In recent times, many of the common law rules developed to protect the health and safety of employees have been incorporated into and supplemented by legislation. The Safety, Health and Welfare at Work Act 1989 is the leading example. As such, a workplace injury claim will also include allegations that the employer failed to comply with his duties under statute. This area of personal injuries is outlined in Chapter 2.

2. Claims for a wrongful or unfair dismissal

A dismissal may be either wrongful or unfair depending on the way in which the employee chooses to pursue his claim to challenge it. A wrongful dismissal is the common law remedy *for a breach of the terms of his employment contract* in the civil courts. An unfair dismissal is a remedy provided specifically by legislation *for a breach of his entitlements under that legislation.*

Injunctions

Where an employee wishes to challenge his dismissal, he may also seek an injunction restraining the alleged breach of his contract of employment and maintaining the *status quo* pending the substantive trial of the dispute. An injunction of this nature may be granted pending the full hearing of a case in circumstances where damages would ***not*** be an adequate remedy were the injunction not granted. This is known as an interlocutory injunction. In order to get such an injunction, an employee must show that there is a fair issue to be tried between the parties and he must give an undertaking as to damages to his employer. This means that he agrees to compensate the injuncted employer in the event that the claim is unsuccessful and where the injunction has caused the employer loss. The court then decides, at its entire discretion and on a balance of convenience between the parties, whether to order such an injunction.

An injunction may also form part of a final order made against an employer at the end of the entire proceedings. This is called a perpetual injunction. However, these are quite rare.

Constructive dismissal

An employee may finally claim that he had no option but to resign his job because his conditions of work became intolerable. In that case, an employee may argue that, since the employer caused or failed to prevent these conditions, that the resignation was, in reality, coerced and he or she was actually dismissed. As such, if successfully proved, this form of resignation is known as **constructive dismissal**. Once again, an employee may challenge this dismissal as either a wrongful or unfair dismissal depending on the forum in which he brings the proceedings.

In such a claim, the burden of proof is on the employee. The employee must also invariably show that he has used or that he sought to invoke the internal grievance procedure within his workplace before he resigned and that this had failed to offer a satisfactory remedy. Once the employee has established, on the face of it, the facts necessary to show that he was forced to resign, the onus then shifts back to the employer to show that he acted reasonably in all the circumstances of the case.

A constructive dismissal claim, albeit an entirely separate relief, may be brought at the same time as and parallel to a personal injuries case. This is because the conduct of an employer or the conditions of work that made the workplace intolerable may also have damaged the state of health of an employee. The entire area of constructive dismissal is dealt with later in Chapter 3.

3. Claims to enforce statutory entitlements where the employer has breached legal rights or protections

In certain circumstances, these claims can be made independently and have their own specific redress and legal forum. Compensation may now be awarded for a breach of these statutory rights as a wrong in itself. This may be the *case even where* no personal injury has yet been suffered or no dismissal has yet occurred or been alleged. The Employment Equality and Labour Relations mechanisms are good examples. This area will be dealt with in the course of Chapters 3 and 4.

One warning

These three areas are **not** mutually exclusive and in most occupational disputes in Ireland today, an employer may be faced with allegations concerning one or more of these claims.

Chapter 2

Occupational Stress: The Final Frontier of Employer Liability?

Understanding the Stress-Related Injury: How the Law sees it?

'Nervous shock:' A Very Victorian affliction

> *"It appears to me to come under the fundamental principles of the law of negligence to hold the defendants liable for reasonably foreseeable psychiatric illness caused by their negligence."*[1]

Some interesting background

It is sometimes not realised that Ireland was one of the first countries in the world to recognise that a person may be held responsible not only for the physical injury that he or she causes another but also for the non-physical injury or psychiatric injury caused.[2] As far back as the late nineteenth century, when the legal systems of Australia and England refused to recognise that a duty of care for such injuries existed, the courts in Ireland accepted that, in the same way that a person may have a duty of care to prevent a person from suffering a physical injury, similarly they may have a duty of care to prevent a psychiatric injury. Eventually, this

---

1 *Mullaly v. Bus Éireann* [1992] I.L.R.M. 722 (High Court), Denham J.

2 McMahon and Binchy, *The Law of Torts*, 3rd Edition (Butterworths, Dublin), p.463.

principle was adopted throughout the rest of the common law world and from that time to today, this type of non-physical injury has been known as '*nervous shock.*'

'Nervous shock': Time to move on?

Nervous shock is a distinct form of injury that refers to the psychiatric effects of a once-off or sudden traumatic event suffered by a person either directly or indirectly. An example of how a person may suffer a trauma indirectly is if he or she witnesses a serious accident.

It is not concerned about protecting mental or psychiatric health as a goal in itself but only with compensating for the psychiatric damage caused by being, directly or indirectly, subjected to a physical trauma or to the imminent risk of such a trauma.

Therefore, in occupational injury claims, it is used primarily where there has been an accident in which an employee either has suffered or was in immediate danger of suffering serious physical injury. In such a case, the employee himself may bring a claim for nervous shock in the event of his suffering a resulting mental injury, or his fellow employees who actually witnessed the accident, may do so.

However, nervous shock is of limited value in giving guidance to an employer for stress, bullying and harassment in the workplace and will not be dealt with in detail in this book.

Firstly, it is of no use to an employee who argues that his mental injuries were suffered not as a result of an individual trauma, such as suffering or witnessing a serious accident, but as a result of a decline in his health over a period of time due to some particular conditions of the workplace with which he or she takes issue. This type of situation is the more important one to claims for stress, bullying or harassment.

Secondly, medical advances have made the state of an individual's mental health more scientifically and clinically ascertainable than ever before and this is particularly important for the cold light of proof required in the courtroom. It has also encouraged the courts to develop the law beyond the limits of nervous shock and to reflect the growth in medical, psychophysical expertise.

Therefore, as a general rule of thumb over the coming years:

> **Employers must be aware that the courts have now accepted the principle that psychiatric health should be protected as a fundamental element of the well-being of an employee, in itself, and that this principle does not depend on any associated occurrence or risk of any physical injury to that employee.**

WORK RELATED MENTAL INJURY: THE THIN END OF THE WEDGE?

> "*Work-related stress is the emotional, cognitive, behavioural and physiological reaction to aversive and noxious aspects of work, work environments and work organisations. It is characterised by high levels of arousal and distress and often by feelings of not coping.*"[3]

Let's banish some myths!

Firstly, pressure at work is not, in itself, unlawful. Nor, of course, should it be. Bullying and harassment, if proved, are, however, unlawful but may not result in a personal injury claim. What the law in recent years has been trying to prevent

---

[3] Farrell Wesley, *The Law of Workplace Stress, Bullying and Harassment*, Bar Review, March/April 2002 per *Guidance on Work Related Stress, Commission of the European Union.*

is instances where employees have suffered mental injury or psychiatric illness as a result of being subjected to such a degree of undue stress in the course of their employment that they can no longer cope and suffer a nervous breakdown or other mental impairment.

Secondly, work-related stress is a symptom of some other failure. It does not exist independently and appear out of nowhere. It is sometimes a failure of the way things are done or sometimes of the people who do them. Trying to eliminate harmful stress is not about pampering employees or about wasting money. At a certain point, stress starts to affect our health. Stress then costs us money. It costs employers money in terms of lost working hours or decreased or substandard production. It costs the entire economy money. That is why harmful stress became and is now an actionable civil wrong. For the victims of bullying and harassment, the stress-related consequences are significant and well established. These include depression, reduced self-esteem, phobias, sleep disturbances, digestive and muscloskeletal problems and post-traumatic stress disorders. These symptoms might persist for years after the incidents. Other established consequences are social isolation and family and financial problems. The legal damages arising from bullying and harassment stress cases can, therefore, be high.

Thirdly, the law does not deal with stress in neat little packages. There is no simple set of rules to work off. Instead, there has been a gradual, often disjointed, accumulation of legal, medical and other professional expertise from which the correct principles can now be distilled. Indeed, it is the very purpose of this publication to do this for employers. Many of the cases that show us how the law will deal with a claim are about workloads and resources and there are very valuable lessons for employers to learn about these in this chapter. But this recent and rapidly developing area of litigation also affects and applies equally to bullying or harassment in the workplace. These also result in harmful stress that injures or impairs our psychiatric health and will be dealt with by the courts and in this chapter in the same way. There is not one law for bullying-related stress, one law for harassment-related stress, another law for other types of harmful stress. In practice, it is all treated in the same way by the courts and as the same area of *work-related* stress. Sometimes, stress is caused by bullying, sometimes by harassment, sometimes by excessive workloads or by a lack of resources. Sometimes, by all of these together. Indeed, sometimes the very instruments of bullying or harassment are the withholding of necessary resources or the imposition of unfair or unreasonable conditions of work.

But, whatever about the style, all too often, the end results are the same: those mental or psychiatric injuries or even suicide.

Who pays?

Workplace Negligence: Difficult Issues of Liability?

Unlike an actual physical injury or wound, a claim relating to stress-related psychiatric injury will pose the courts far more difficulty.

Diagnosis

Firstly, a court will have to establish if there is a psychiatric illness or injury at all and, if so, what that illness is. Work-related stress, itself, is not a disease or illness but rather it leads to disease or illness. Therefore, in seeking civil damages, an employee must do more than simply allege his or her exposure to work-related stress. At common law, at least, a psychiatric illness or injury is one that must lend itself to clinical diagnosis and scrutiny. This is a conclusion that the trial judge will draw based on the particular expert medical reports and evidence examined and cross-examined in the course of the proceedings.

Work-related stress: A vicious circle?

Secondly, a court will have to establish the blame for any illness. A question that may obviously be asked is whether an alleged occupational mental injury was a psychological condition inherent in the employee all along and only exacerbated by the responsibilities of his employment. Also, it may be the case that an employee may be suffering from stress or mental upset not related to his work and outside of the work environment. In that case, it may not be clear if an employer is entirely liable or even liable at all in the event of his employee suffering a purported psychiatric injury in the workplace.

These are all valid points and the law is very mindful of their implications. In one of the most important recent cases on work-related stress, it was stated:

> "[T]he relationship between work conditions and depressive illness is potentially complex ... [S]tressful working conditions can cause a person to develop a depressive illness. Conversely ... depressive illness can adversely affect a person's ability to cope with his work. There can develop ... a vicious circle or vicious cycle in which the more depressed a person becomes, the worse he performs at work and the more he perceives that he is performing badly at work, the worse his depression becomes. When the matter comes to be investigated once the depression is established, it is very difficult to break into the cycle and identify where it began."[4]

---

[4] *Cross v. Highlands and Islands Enterprises* [2001] I.R.L.R. 336 *per* Lord Macfadyen at p. 348.

Each case will ultimately be dealt with on the basis of its own merits and the issue as to where any particular threshold may lie will depend on the circumstances and facts of the particular situation.

How these circumstances and facts are measured depends on the following principles of law.

THE CONCEPT OF REASONABLENESS: ALL THINGS TO ALL PEOPLE?

General overview

As referred to in Chapter 1, the test of reasonableness is the cornerstone of the common law and the tort of negligence is no exception. This simply means that the actions of a party to proceedings will be assessed in order to decide if they acted reasonably or not. The law does not attach any specific meaning to the word 'reasonable', it is merely a device created by the courts to allow them to balance the subjective arguments of the parties before them as to *what they did* against a more objective perspective of *what they should have done*.

Nevertheless, although it has been expressed in different ways over the past 150 years, what is clear and settled law today is that an employer owes an employee a duty of care in the workplace.

This means that *an employer must take all* ***reasonable steps*** *to protect an employee from risks or hazards to health and safety in the course of his employment that are* ***reasonably foreseeable*** *in all the circumstances of the case.*

'Reasonable steps'

An employer's duty is not an absolute one.

An employer cannot and is not expected to adopt the role of insurer and be required to take precautions against every conceivable form of risk no matter what the cost and no matter how remote that risk may be.

The employer is only expected to behave as a reasonable and prudent employer would have done *at the time* in all the circumstances of the case.[5]

Hindsight is not a '*darling of the civil courts*.'

It is equally the case that the concept of reasonableness will vary from case to case.

What is reasonable in any particular case will depend on the following four factors: [6]

(i) The nature of the employment relationship between the parties;

(ii) The magnitude of the risk of injury that was reasonably foreseeable;

(iii) The seriousness of the consequences of the injury for the employee;

(iv) The costs and practicability of preventing the risk.

The nature of the employment relationship

The nature of the relationship simply refers to the age, seniority and level of knowledge and experience of the employee. The more junior or inexperienced an employee, the greater the duty of care an employee owes to him or her.

The magnitude of risk

Quite clearly, an employer must have regard to the likelihood, degree and scale of a risk of work-related stress and/or bullying or harassment.

---

5 *Christie v. Odeon (Ireland) Limited* (1957) 91 I.L.T.R. 25.

6 *Walker v. Northumberland County Council* [1995] All E.R. 737.

The seriousness of the consequences

An employer must have regard to the seriousness of its consequences in taking the precautions required to protect against employees. This is separate to the above in that it considers the aftermath of any injury rather than the risk factors leading up to the injury.

The costs and practicalities

Finally, the costs and practicalities of the precautions required are also important. Therefore, even if an employer *knew* of a risk or hazard in a particular case that has caused his employee injury, then he or she is entitled to defend the failure to take precautions against it on the basis that the necessary costs and practicalities they involved were so onerous as to be prohibitive and unreasonable. [7]

This may be validly the case where the seriousness or likelihood of a risk is so outweighed by the costs or disruption to the business in preventing it that it would be disproportionate to the benefit achieved. In the specific context of the risk of work-related stress, the following practicalities are important.

(a) The size of the business. The larger an organisation, the heavier the duty a court may place on it. This is because there was a greater opportunity to safely distribute the workload;

(b) The resources available to an employer to take precautions;

(c) The need to be fair to other employees in the redistribution of any work. The smaller the workforce, the more important this factor becomes;

---

[7] *Bradley v. CIE* [1976] I.R. 217 (SC).

(d) Whether the business is subject to seasonal fluctuations in terms of workload: the 'all hands on deck' explanation. Or, are stress related working conditions a regular feature or even a tool of how employees are treated in the workplace?

Moreover, it must also be borne in mind that where the magnitude of a risk or the seriousness of its consequences are so great as to lead to death or serious physical injury, the less importance the courts attach to the costs and practicality arguments of an employer.[8] Similarly, the more serious the risk and the consequences to the mental health of an employee up to and including the risks of suicide, the less likely these excuses will be entertained. Moreover, the more entrenched the concepts of occupational stress, bullying and harassment become among the judiciary, the higher the threshold before an employer will be permitted to succeed in using cost and practicality arguments to rebut them.

'Reasonably foreseeable'

General principles

A reasonably foreseeable risk is one of which an employer knew or ought to have known prior to the injury being sustained.

- The onus is on the employee to prove what the employer knew or ought to have known.
- The requisite standard of proof in civil law cases is the balance of probabilities. This is at a level normally greater than a 50/50 chance.

---

8 *Daly v. Avonmore Creameries Limited* [1984] I.R. 131 (SC) *per* McCarthy J.

- This is significantly less than the criminal standard where a case must be proved beyond a reasonable doubt.

What an employer *ought* to have known is a problematic issue. This is because all civil wrongs are subject to a threshold across which the courts will not go in blaming a defendant for an accident. When an employee fails to prove that his employer did know or ought to have known of a risk, the injury complained of is deemed to be too far removed from the act or omission alleged to have been the cause of that injury. This is the case even where it is ultimately found that the plaintiff has indeed suffered the injury as alleged.

This is of particular importance in the case of risks or hazards of purely non-physical injury arising out of stress, bullying or harassment in the course of employment. This is due to the fact that, in these cases, an employee has to do more than simply prove that his employer foresaw a risk or some risk of a personal injury generally. He has to prove that his employer foresaw an actual and specific risk of mental or psychiatric injury ultimately suffered by the employee. This is a higher standard than proving risks to physical injury *simpliciter*.

Important Signposts to the Future of Employer Liability in Ireland

Walker v. Northumberland County Council: Lightning never strikes twice?[9]

Background

This is an English case from 1995. Mr Walker was a social worker employed with a county council and was responsible

---

9 [1995] All E.R. 737.

for and manager of four teams of fieldworkers concerned with childcare in his allocated region. Initially the region was a mixed rural and urban one but over the years, the area over which he was responsible became increasingly populated and urbanised. However, resources allocated to him failed to keep up with demand in terms of staff and financial requirements. Moreover, the nature of the work being handled by Mr Walker was distressful and emotionally draining. As a result, in 1986, he suffered a nervous breakdown due to occupational stress and the pressures and burdens of work.

He took sick leave for three months. Before he returned to work, he had asked his employer and was assured that the burden would be decreased and that appropriate resources would be allocated to him. However, when he returned, the promises made failed to materialise and six months later he suffered a second nervous breakdown. This second breakdown resulted in his permanently ceasing to work for the defendant. He was dismissed by his employer on the grounds of permanent ill-health.

Mr Walker issued a personal injury action on the basis that his employer had failed to provide him with a safe system of work and that it had failed to take reasonable steps to prevent his nervous breakdowns.

The decision

The court held that the defendant was not responsible for the first nervous breakdown. This was because it neither knew nor ought to have known that Mr Walker's workload exposed him to a material risk of mental injury. However, the situation changed radically after he returned to work following the first breakdown. At that point, the employer knew or ought to have known that if the employee's workload was not decreased and the necessary resources allocated to him, then he was exposed to a risk of another nervous breakdown that would end his career with them. In other words, the employer reasonably foresaw that its employee was now exposed to a materially higher risk of mental injury. Therefore, the employer was responsible for the second nervous breakdown and was liable in negligence for the damage.

The lessons of Walker: A case of less known the better?

Psychiatric damage

This case recognises that, as a general rule, **psychiatric damage** should be considered as a breach of an employer's duty of care to his employees just like any physical injury would. The interesting thing about this case is that the level of work and sources of occupational stress were the same prior to both breakdowns. In other words, the work environment and conditions were the same throughout both periods. Yet, the employer was only liable for the second breakdown. Why?

Vulnerability

The reason for this is that it was only on the second occasion that the employer was aware or ought to have been aware that Walker was a **vulnerable employee** and exposed to suffering a nervous breakdown.

Working conditions

This approach takes the spotlight off **the actual stress-related working conditions** and environment (whether through work levels, harassment or bullying) and places it fully on the nature of the injury the employee is claiming to have suffered.

As a result of the first breakdown, it was held that he was exposed to a risk of mental injury that was **materially higher** than that which would normally affect a person in his position. It appears that it was only at this point that the employer ought to have been aware that it should have done something.

What is meant by 'materially higher' will depend on the particular facts of each case.

No independent duty of care to avoid stressful working conditions

Under this decision, an employer could arguably impose whatever **working conditions** it likes on its employees, however pressurised or hostile, so long as there is nothing to show that it was aware or ought to have been aware of any of them suffering psychiatrically.

To use a building analogy, the employer may not be negligent for building a structure with bad foundations but for failing to spot the cracks in the walls before it subsides!

As such, there was no duty of care on an employer to prevent him or her from imposing hostile or overly pressurised working conditions as a wrong in itself. This, after all, was what led up to Walker's first breakdown for which his employer escaped blame.

These principles remain the rule so long as the *Walker* test is applied.

Strong employer protection

It provides **strong protection for an employer**. This also provides an employer with a defence to some of the concerns outlined in this chapter as to the differences in tolerance levels among employees to stress whether it be caused by heavy workloads, bullying or harassment.

Did or should employer know

Finally, it means that, even if an employee proves that he or she **has suffered** mental illness or injury through **harassment or bullying in the workplace**, that may still not be enough to win his or her case for damages, unless he can also prove that the illness or injury was one that the employer knew or ought to have known.

> It seemed a case of 'the less known the better'.

This approach has been overtaken by professional health and safety practice and research. Moreover, it is doubtful that this is the law in all cases. An important recent case now confirms this.

Cross v. Highlands and Island Enterprises: **Working conditions can kill!**[10]

Background

This is a decision reported in 2001. Mr Cross was a senior training manager who suffered from anxiety or work-related stress. This included:

- Feelings of inability to cope with his job,
- Anxiety about the future,
- Difficulty in concentrating and
- Sleep disturbance.

These were symptoms that Mr Cross attributed to work-related problems that included:

- Too great a workload;
- A lack of assistance;
- An inadequate availability of secretarial help.

---

[10] [2001] I.R.L.R. 336.

In the month of April 1993, his doctor certified him as unfit to work for a month due to stress. In May 1993, he was so certified for another month. In June 1993, he was certified as fit to return to work.

When he returned his workload was lightened and he was allocated work of a more procedural nature rather than work that called for investigation and preparation of reports. In August 1993, Mr Cross committed suicide and his family sought damages on the grounds that his suicide was due to work related stress.

The decision

The court held that the employer here was not liable as it had not breached its duty of care to Mr Cross. This was because the employer, unlike in *Walker*, had taken reasonable care on his return to reduce his workload.

This decision not only applies *Walker* but affirms it as an appropriate test. However, in so doing, it has expanded the scope of an employer's duty of care. It has potentially profound and far-reaching effects for employer liability. It is little wonder, therefore, that it has been reported as the 'breakthrough decision' on stress at work in the United Kingdom.[11] Therefore, for all Irish employers, the following points decided in *Cross* should be particularly noted:

- If it had been established that, before he became depressed, James Cross was struggling to cope with a job which placed on him responsibilities, the nature and scope of which, were beyond his capacity and experience and for which he was inadequately trained; that the staff resources available to him, including secretarial and administrative support, were inadequate; and the resulting difficulties were compounded by the humiliating experience of having his work regularly

---

[11] [2001] I.R.L.R. 322.

and repeatedly rejected by the chief executive, and then, when finalised, rejected or subjected to unreasonable criticism by members of the board, it might have been reasonable to conclude that it was probably those stressful circumstances that *precipitated the depression* rather than depression that led him to feel that he was not coping with his job.[12]

- It would be unacceptable for the law to adopt a position which meant that an employer who knew without doubt that the conditions in which he required an employee to work were so stressful that it was objectively likely that, *over time, the employee would succumb to psychiatric illness*, and, nevertheless continued to subject the employee to those conditions, despite growing signs that he was developing such psychiatric illness, would incur no liability for the loss and damage suffered by the employee as a result of developing the psychiatric illness.[13]

Walker or Cross: A case of nature versus nurture?

Employer must protect psychiatric health of employees

In the first instance an employer must now protect and prevent injury to the psychiatric health of his employees. Where a particular employee has a specific vulnerability or there is a specific risk of mental injury to him that an employer knew or he ought to have been aware of in the circumstances, then he is liable for an injury. When an employee is *returning from sick-leave* due to a stress-related illness, an employer must deal with the particular workplace problems that this employee has expressed to him that cause or may exacerbate the illness or that the employer believes that that employee

---

[12] *Op. cit.*, 337.
[13] *Op. cit.*, 348.

may encounter into the future. However, this process will be rooted in the particular circumstances of the employee returning to work and what he or she needs. According to *Cross*, an employer, at this point, will not have to embark on a general exploration of the system or place of work to find and prevent every possible or potential source of stress.

However, the court then went further.

Independent duty of care to avoid hazardous working condition

Secondly in *Cross*, the court explicitly said that employers have a duty to take reasonable care not to subject the employees to **working conditions** that are reasonably foreseeably likely to cause them psychiatric injury or illness.

This is the biggest difference from *Walker* where no such duty was independently recognised. Indeed, this judgment may have been designed to deliberately close that loophole. In *Walker*, the reasonableness of working conditions depended entirely on what an employer knew or ought to have known about the individual susceptibility of the employee at risk. There was no objective standard to measure the working conditions themselves. This objective standard is precisely what has been introduced in *Cross*.

It now casts the net wider and this means that an employer can now be blamed irrespective of his or her state of knowledge of the employee's personal vulnerabilities or susceptibilities if the conditions of work themselves are found to be negligent. Once an employee complains about the stressful nature of certain aspects of his working conditions, for whatever reason, an employer is very well advised, unless the complaint is clearly frivolous or vexatious, at the very least, to take the complaint seriously, to set about inquiring into the matter raised by it and, if substantiated, to take firm and effective remedial action.

If this approach had been applied in *Walker*, it is quite

likely that the employer would have been liable for the first breakdown as well as the second. The importance of the decision in *Cross* for employers is that the risk of psychiatric injury caused by workplace stress may now be considered as an *environmental* risk that may be assessed and not merely a medical one intrinsic to a particular employee. In simple terms, it is something like a risk of exposure to noxious fumes that an employer must prevent all employees from.

In other words, the common law seems to now accept that stress-induced injury can be both something in the *nature* of the employee or it can be something *nurtured* by his environment. Not so much a case of nature *versus* nurture but a case of nature *and* nurture!

As such, this decision brings the law into line with general occupational health and safety practice that views stress as an environmental risk.[14] It also brings the common law view of work-related stress a further step closer to the approach increasingly being taken by statutory and industrial relations bodies (see below).

Risk assessments

Legislation provides that every employer must prepare a statement in writing for his workplace known as a 'safety statement'. This statement has to be based on an identification of the hazards and an assessment of the risks to health and safety at the place of work to which the safety statement relates.[15] When this legislation was introduced, a general duty of care to protect psychiatric health (as distinct from just nervous shock) had not yet been recognised by the common law. Therefore, the question arises as to whether the obligations of health and safety legislation, such as a risk

---

[14] Health and Safety Authority of Ireland, *Health and Safety Matters*, Newsletter, Summer, 2002, p. 8.

[15] Section 12 of the Safety, Health and Welfare at Work Act 1989.

assessment, cover the protection of mental health in the workplace also.

In keeping with the cautiousness of the common law, the court, in *Cross*, did not go so far as to hold that the defendant should have carried out **an actual health and safety assessment of the risks of work-related stress** in the same way as required for the risks of physical injuries. This was simply because the court believed, as a matter of fact, that, in the past, employers had never been so required to carry out a risk assessment in relation to the risks of psychiatric harm either in general or in the specific case of an employee returning to work after an illness. The court stated that this remained the case up to the time of the suicide of Mr Cross in 1993.

However, the refusal to recognise that an employer had a duty of care to prepare a risk assessment was not an outright one. It was simply based, firstly, on the *general perception* of employers in 1993 that this obligation did not bear upon the specific risks of psychiatric illness and, secondly, it was not then *normal practice* to make mental health the subject of a formal assessment. Interestingly, the court declined to express a view as to what is proper practice now.

However, what is clear is that, since 1993, when Mr Cross committed suicide, it is now a matter of law that employers are liable for the mental health of their employees in the workplace. Moreover, substantial volumes of professional and governmental guidelines and publications have been targeted, in recent years, at employers regarding the effects and consequences of work-related stress. In addition, legislation and codes of practice providing for the well-being of employees over and above merely their physical health have been introduced. Finally, the very outcome of *Cross* itself, by connecting stressful working conditions directly to liability for stress-induced illness, (without necessarily any intervening specific and reasonably foreseeable mental vulnerability to the employee), now reinforces the need of employers to take preventative measures in line with those more familiar to them in the realm of physical healthcare. As discussed later in this chapter, normal health and safety practice and the general perception of mental health have changed significantly. As such, the law, although a slower beast, equally expects that a reasonable and prudent employer would keep up with and adopt such developments. Furthermore, even if an employer does not do so, such information will be considered as something he ought to have known anyway! In particular, this approach of the common law to development and change may be explained by the following passage that was recently relied on in a bullying and harassment case in Ireland:

> "...where there is a recognised and general practice which has been followed for a substantial period of time in similar circumstances, without mishap, [an employer] is entitled to follow it, unless in the light of common sense or newer knowledge, it is clearly bad; but, where there is developing knowledge, he must keep reasonably abreast of it and not be too slow to apply it; and where he has, in fact, greater than average knowledge of the risks, he may be thereby obliged to take more than then average or standard precautions."[16]

Therefore, on the *Cross* criteria and test alone, risk assessments specifically inclusive of the risks of work-related stress and of psychiatric injury generally, might now be the unavoidable, if not yet entirely mandatory, means by which an employer may seek to minimise possible exposure to such

---

[16] *Stokes v. Guest, Keen and Nettlefold (Bolts and Nuts) Limited* [1968] 1 W.L.R. 1776 as cited with approval in *Browne v. Ventelo Telecommunications (Irl) Limited,* UD 597/2001, July 16, 2002.

claims. Rather than deal with issues concerning work-related stress in a piece-meal fashion as they arise, a formal assessment in writing of the risks of work-related stress would provide an employer with the tools to significantly prevent the problem ever arising in the first place. Moreover, if employees do not complain but instead endure, by the time an employer or management may recognise the symptoms of work-related stress in the workforce, the damage may already have been done whereas with a risk assessment they may have spotted and prevented it on time. Finally, the existence of such an effective and implemented risk assessment is an important defence for any stress-related personal injury claim in the civil courts.

So, why are these UK cases so important?

UK cases are obviously not directly applied in Ireland and it is never absolutely certain that Irish judgments will not deviate somewhat from them where they are applied. However, the approach of the Irish courts to date has indicated that there is no reason why a *Walker* type of approach will not be followed here and indeed they already appear to have applied its principles in Ireland. Moreover, the general principles of negligence law are common to the jurisdictions of both the UK and Ireland. As such, a growing number of Irish cases indicate that courts here are also increasingly persuaded by the specific reasoning that has proven so influential in the UK in cases relating to occupational stress injuries.

Firstly, in 2000, a reported judgment of the Circuit Court explicitly confirmed the willingness of the Irish judiciary to move beyond a traditional 'nervous shock' view of psychiatric illness and follow *Walker* and its reasoning.[17]

---

[17] *Curran v. Cadbury (Ireland) Limited* [2000] 2 I.L.R.M. 343.

Secondly, in 1999, the High Court in Ireland, even prior to *Cross*, provided a signal that such an approach would be followed here over the coming years.

McHugh v. The Minister for Defence. Combating trauma: stress on the frontline[18]

The background

This case involved a failure of the defendant to recognise or treat the obvious symptoms of a stress-related psychiatric injury suffered by the plaintiff. It was set in the extreme conditions of frontline Irish military peacekeeping in the Lebanon in which the plaintiff, during his tour of duty, was exposed to a series of distressing incidents including his witnessing the dead bodies of other soldiers.

The judgment

The decision, based on the starkest of situations rather than the conventional workplace, is, nonetheless, valuable in that the principles it relies on are based on the general duty of care of employers to protect the health and safety of their employees. As such, it is equally significant to other instances of work-related stress. It demonstrates the attitude of the High Court to such injuries in Ireland. In particular, the court stated:

> "...the defendant owed to the plaintiff a duty to take reasonable care for the health and safety of the plaintiff. In my view there was a negligent failure to take appropriate care for the health of the plaintiff in that once he became subject to stress, which was likely to happen and was

---

[18] High Court, January 28, 1999 *per* Budd J.

> reasonably foreseeable in the dangerous and macabre situations in the Lebanon, the defendants failed to spot the obvious manifestations of post-traumatic stress or else negligently failed to recognise the significance of the symptoms and also failed to obtain remedial therapy for the plaintiff."

The lessons?

This is a very wide duty indeed. It means that an employer is negligent not only if he *does* spot an injury or *does* recognise its symptoms and nonetheless fails to intervene but also if he *does not* actually know or genuinely recognise particular symptoms relating to a work-related psychiatric illness in circumstances where a court considers that he *ought to have known*. What these circumstances are will depend on the merits of each case. As such, it must be borne in mind that this decision arose out of the extreme circumstances of the Lebanon.

Nevertheless, this case is very important because it shows that the Irish High Court is willing to look to the *working conditions* of employees in order to assess the reasonableness of the employer in the circumstances of a situation rather than merely the individual susceptibility of the employee. In other words, the *Cross* test as well as the *Walker* one. The High Court did not limit itself to considering whether the plaintiff had a particular vulnerability or not which the defendant ought to have been aware of. Indeed, the whole assumption of the decision is that it was not so aware. Instead, it simply said that, since the '*dangerous and macabre situations*' of work themselves were reasonably foreseeably likely to lead to stress, then the defendant came under a duty to act.

In simple terms, since the defendant in this case knew or ought to have known that the conditions of work might be stressful when assessed objectively, it, therefore, had a duty of care to act to prevent them.

Once again, on the basis of the approach of this Irish decision, the undertaking of a specific risk assessment for work-related stress identifying the sources and preventing its effects, as already discussed in this chapter, would go a significant way in ensuring that an employer does not fail to identify or spot the risks and symptoms of stress-related injury in his workplace.

With this in mind, and given the past trend of the incorporation generally into Ireland of the reasoning of decisions from the UK, there is a significant likelihood that a *Cross* style refinement to *Walker* may also be introduced here. After all, *Cross* does not deviate from Walker, it simply comes to the same conclusion from a different angle. It plugs a gap left by the *Walker* decision. The principles underpinning both are mostly similar and the Irish courts are willing not only to follow *Walker*, as expressed in the Circuit Court, but also to look at stressful working conditions as well as vulnerabilities as shown in the High Court.

However, in the meantime, while awaiting the definitive view of the Irish courts, employers should, at the very least, be particularly mindful of what *Walker* and *Cross* say and their implications.

Present law in Ireland: A work in progress?

Therefore, the present law in Ireland may be summarised as the following:

Vulnerability test

If an employee can prove that his employer knew or ought to have known of *a specific risk of a psychiatric injury or illness* to him as a result of a risk or hazard that his employer created or failed to prevent, then the employer will be liable for that injury or illness. This test is underpinned by what a reasonable and prudent employer would do in the particular circumstances of the susceptible employee (either at work or returning to work) rather than motivated by any general duty of care relating to working conditions generally.

Working conditions test

If *the working conditions are such that an employer knew that they were likely, when looked at objectively, to cause such illness or injury* and he failed to take reasonable steps to prevent that from happening then he may now also be liable for such injury or illness under the *Cross* and *McHugh* decisions. What an employer knew or ought to have known can be assessed with reference to the nature of a particular environment and the industry, professional or other government guidelines and publications available on stress and psychiatric injury in the workplace.

Employers must always be aware that this is an area that is developing very quickly and decisions and guidelines are emerging apace that have a bearing on application of the above rules. Therefore, it is essential that HR and Personnel managers and staff are aware of innovations and best practice on stress induced injuries in the workplace at all times.

Best practice specifically for bullying and harassment are set out in Chapters 3 and 4.

Present law in the U.K.: A glimpse into the future?

To facilitate employers in this increasingly complex area, the Court of Appeal in England, at an opportune time, in February 2002, has now delivered a comprehensive set of guidelines and principles on best practice at common law relating to work related stress. These guidelines, it will be noticed, are essentially a marriage of the *Walker* type principles and those of *Cross*.

Of course, although these guidelines arose in the context of the burden of pressurised workloads, they may be applied by analogy to stress induced mental injuries caused by other work conditions such as the bullying or harassment of an employee by his employer or fellow employees. These are equally likely to result in the conditions that cause stress induced mental injuries.

Moreover, although the Irish courts themselves have yet to provide Irish employers with a similar set of guidelines, many of the principles below, it is suggested, are likely to be applied in Ireland.

Therefore, in the meantime, as with *Cross*, while we await a decision in Ireland, employers should err on the side of caution and be very mindful of these guidelines.

Sixteen Golden Rules: The Case of Sutherland v. Hatton; Somerset County v. Barber; Sandwell Metropolitan Borough Council v. Jones; Baker Refractories Limited v. Bishop[19]

Duty

1. There are no special or distinct legal restrictions applying to claims for psychiatric illness or injury arising from the stress of doing work the employee is required to do. The ordinary principles of employer's liability apply.

Foreseeability

2. Is the kind of harm to a particular employee reasonably foreseeable? This has two components: (a). An injury to

---

[19] February 5, 2002, Court of Appeal, (Hale, Brooke, Kay LJJ.), [2002] E.W.C.A. Civ. 76. Farrell Welsey, *The Law of Workplace Stress, Bullying and Harassment,* 7 Bar Review June/July 2002, 254.

health; (b). is attributable to stress at work (as distinct from other factors).

3. Whether an employer foresees an injury depends on what the employer knows (or ought reasonably to know) about the individual employee. Because of the nature of mental disorder, it is harder to foresee than physical injury, but may be easier to foresee in a known individual rather than the population at large. An employer is usually entitled to assume that the employee can withstand the normal pressures of the job unless he knows of some particular problem or vulnerability.

4. The test is the same whatever the employment. There are no occupations that should be regarded as intrinsically dangerous to mental health.

5. Factors likely to be relevant in answering at what point an employer's liability kicks in are:

- (a) The nature and extent of the work done by the employee.
  - (i) Is the workload much more than is normal for the particular job?
  - (ii) Is the work particularly intellectually or emotionally demanding for this employee?
  - (iii) Are the demands being made of this employee unreasonable or excessive when compared with the demands of other employees in the same or comparable jobs?
  - (iv) Are there signs that others doing this job are suffering harmful levels of stress?
  - (v) Is there an abnormal level of sickness or absenteeism in the same job or the same department?
- (b) Signs from the employees of impending harm to health.
  - (i) Has he a particular problem or vulnerability?

(ii) Has he already suffered an illness attributable to stress at work.

(iii) Has there recently been frequent or prolonged absences which are uncharacteristic of him?

(iv) Is there reason to believe that these are attributable to stress at work, for example, because of complaints or warnings from him or others?

6. The employer is generally entitled to take what he is told by his employee at face value, unless he has good reason to think to the contrary. He generally does not have to make searching enquiries of the employee or to seek his permission to make further enquiries of his medical advisers.

7. To trigger a duty to take steps, the indications of impending harm to health arising from stress at work must be plain enough for any reasonable employer to realise that he should do something.

Breach of duty

8. The employer is only in breach of duty if he has failed to take the steps which are reasonable in the circumstances, bearing in mind the magnitude of the risk of harm occurring, the gravity of the actual harm that may occur, the costs and practicality of preventing it and the justifica-tions for running the risk.

9. The size and scope of the employer's business, its resources and the demands it faces are relevant in deciding what are reasonable. These include the interests of other employees and the need to treat them fairly, for example, in any redistribution of duties.

10. The employer can only reasonably be expected to take steps that are likely to do some good. The court is likely to need expert evidence on this.

11. An employer who offers a confidential advice service, with referral to appropriate counselling or treatment services, is unlikely to be found in breach of duty.

12. If the only reasonable and effective step would have been to dismiss and demote an employee, the employer will not be in breach of duty in allowing a willing employee to continue in his job.

13. In all cases, a court will identify the steps that the employer could and should have taken before finding him in breach of duty.

Causation

14. The claimant employee must show that the breach of duty has caused or materially contributed to the harm suffered. It is not enough to merely show that occupational stress has caused the harm.

Apportionment and quantification of damages

15. Where the harm suffered has more than one cause, the employer should only pay for that proportion of the harm suffered that is attributable to his wrongdoing, unless the harm is truly indivisible. It is for the employer defendant to raise the question of apportionment.

16. The assessment of damages will take account of any pre-existing disorder or vulnerability and of the chance that the claimant would have succumbed to a stress-related disorder quite apart from the workplace. Similarly, the issue of any contributory negligence of the employee will have an influence on the damages awarded.

Precautions: how to limit your liability against stress claims

The risk assessment: prevention is better than cure!

As seen in the above cases, negligence law is only concerned with preventing injuries or damage to employees caused by work-related stress as a result of the default of employers. On the other hand, most recent health and safety practice is broader in its aims and seeks to eliminate stress from the workplace altogether. As we have seen there is no liability at common law for an employer simply because a court finds his workplace is one where there is occupational stress levels.

However, the lower the occurrence of occupational stress in the business, the less likely it is that it will ever reach the point of inflicting a personal injury and of threatening the health of its employees at all. Moreover, employers are increasingly exposed to compensation claims for work-related stress on grounds other than established by the common law.[20] Therefore, employers should approach this area from the perspective of not simply trying to do enough to avoid basic liability for personal injury claims at common law but of minimising their exposure to liability altogether. The best way to do this is to develop their practices by analogy with the broader aims of the health and safety profession. If this is done, the employer gets the best of both worlds.

Also, don't forget the *Cross* decision relies on the changes in the general perception and normal practice of employers towards psychiatric injury in deciding whether there is now a duty of care to prepare a risk assessment!

Therefore, both a good health and safety practice and a good litigation avoidance strategy go arm in arm. **Employers be ambitious!** In order to compete in the labour market both now and into the future, employers should be building up

---

[20] See Chapter 3.

team-work and loyalty to the business among their employees. Destructive work environments damage not only the health and safety of the employees who suffer but they further undermine and damage the business and the investments made in the training and recruiting of staff.

How to go about assessing an invisible risk: is it all in the mind?

Firstly, employers should seek to minimise stress in the same way as they would highly visible risks like toxins and chemicals. In other words, approach it from the same risk management and control ethos already developed to prevent risks to physical injuries. Health and Safety best practice states that the assessment of risk for work-related stress involves the same basic principles and process as for any other workplace hazard. In other words, stress may be identified and assessed in a similar, technical way. It isn't just all in the mind!

Secondly, work should involve **a properly organised programme of activities** designed both to satisfy the needs of the customers and marketplace as well as the individual needs of an employee.[21] Controls on the workplace should involve both the **policies** and the **systems** in place to implement them.

Policies include any written documents, regulations, workplace rules and 'accepted' workplace practice provided by the employer to his employees.

Systems are needed, in order to enforce such policies, and an employer may either have to implement new or change some of his or her prior workplace systems.

Thirdly, employers should be aware that certain type of work environments have been found to be more stress inducing than others:

---

[21] Above at fn 8, p.8.

- High pressure, short-time frame, tight target jobs;
- Jobs with constantly high workloads with no ease-off periods;
- Mundane repetitive work with no peaks or immediate goals;
- Jobs where there is a threat of physical/sexual violence;
- Jobs where there is bullying and harassment;
- Jobs where highly complex decisions must regularly be made.[22]

The employees and their representatives should be included in this process in order to enhance its success. They should be asked what are the sources of stress, which groups are suffering and what can be done to help.

What do I have to do and how far do I go?

The steps of risk assessment in the context of work related stress, are[23]:

1. Identify the hazards

Risk factors to look out for are:

Organisational culture or atmosphere
Are there poor communication levels, low levels of support for problem solving and personal development, lack of definition of organisational objectives?

---

22 Above at fn. 14, p.7.

23 European Agency for Safety and Health at Work, Research on Work Related Stress, 2000, Cox T., Griffiths A., Rial-Gonzalez E.; 'FACTS, European Agency for Safety and Health at Work, Summary of Agency Report,' Bulletin 8, Summer 2002.

Decision latitude/control

How much influence do workers have in the way they do their work? Are there low participation rates in decision-making or a lack of control over work?

Interpersonal relationships at work

Is there social or physical isolation of individual or groups of employees, poor relationships with superiors, a lack of social support, interpersonal conflict such as bullying and harassment?

Role in the organisation

Do the employees clearly understand their role in the organisation and is conflict or ambiguity in their roles avoided? Do more senior employees/managers with a responsibility for people understand their role in the organisation and their role in applying the policies and guidelines of an employer?

Change in the workplace

How do you manage and communicate the organisational changes you make in the workplace?

Career development

Are their feelings of career stagnation or uncertainty among employees? Is there under or over promotion? Are employees concerned about poor pay, job insecurity or a low social value attached to their work?

Task design

Is there a lack of variety or short work cycles? Is work fragmented or meaningless? Is there an underuse of skills? Are employees properly trained to perform the tasks? Is there high uncertainty as to how or what tasks are assigned to employees?

Workload/workplace

Is there work overload, a lack of control over pacing, high levels of time pressure, a lack of or no clearly defined supports available?

Work schedules

Is attention paid to the particular requirements of shift workers? Are there inflexible work schedules generally? Are there unpredictable working hours? Are there long and unsocial working hours?

2. Decide who might be harmed

An employer may identify an employee under severe stress (that is, stress likely to result in litigation) if he or she is behaving in one or more of the following ways:

- Being prone to tearfulness, impulsiveness and out-of-character behaviour;
- Being aggressive and irritable without apparent cause;
- Becoming a bully or harasser;
- Having disciplinary problems or becoming isolated;
- Showing poor levels of concentration and focus;
- Developing a variety of illnesses or conditions not medically explained;
- Reduced productivity, poor decision-making, unusual errors;
- Exhibit tired, lethargic, apathetic behaviour;
- Develop dependencies on alcohol, drugs, people;
- Lose interest in many aspects of life within and outside work.[24]

---

[24] Above at fn. 14; FACTS, European Agency for Safety and Health at Work, Work-Related Stress, Bulletin 22, Belgium 2002.

3. Evaluate the risk by

(a) Identifying what action has already been taken;

(b) Deciding whether this is enough;

(c) If it is not, deciding what more should be done.

Culture
Are there good, open communication skills, support and mutual respect? Are the views of workers and their representatives valued? If not, communication skills should be improved, particularly for staff working remotely.

Demands
Are staff overloaded? Do they have the capabilities and competence for their tasks? What about the physical (noise, vibration, ventilation, lighting) and psychosocial (bullying, harassment, violence) environments? Sufficient resources should be made available if there are problems. The working day should be structured or re-structured e.g. tasks should be re-prioritised. The intensity of the workload should be reduced. Staff training should enable people to carry out their tasks competently.

Control
Do individuals have sufficient say in the way their work is carried out? Staff should have control to plan their own work, to make decisions about how that work should be completed and how to solve problems. Jobs should be enriched as much as possible so that staff can use their skills to advantage. A supportive environment is crucial. Workers should be provided with regular goals and feedback.

Relationships

How are relationships between colleagues and between colleagues and managers? What about the relationship between managers and senior managers? Is there evidence of any bullying or harassment? Procedures should be available such as disciplinary and grievance procedures to deal with unacceptable behaviour. A culture should be developed where staff trust each other and recognise each other's contributions. Once again, good and interpersonal communication skills should form part of the quality a manager or supervisor brings to his job and this skill should be nurtured and encouraged among the workers themselves.

Change

Are workers anxious about their employment status? Are they confused about workplace changes and what it means for them? Are there changes that could be made in the design of work tasks or structures that would help employees alleviate unnecessary stress? Clear communication helps before, during and after change. Also, giving staff the chance to influence change makes them feel more involved, secure and less anxious about the future (a major source of workplace stress as identified in the court cases earlier).

Role

Do people suffer role conflict (conflicting demands) or role ambiguity (lack of definition or clarity)? Staff should have clearly defined roles and responsibilities. Staff should be aware when they are going outside these.

Support, training and individual factors

Is there adequate induction for new recruits and staff

whose jobs have changed? Are staff given social support? Is account taken of individual differences, e.g., some members may thrive on working to tight deadlines; others may like time to plan. Is it really necessary to always work to tight deadlines, e.g., is it something structural to the nature of the business or something that has simply always been done in that way?

Staff should be supported, given feedback and encouraged, even when things go wrong. Involve staff and value their diversity. Workplace health promotion activities should be encouraged along with a healthy work/private life balance. Do you encourage or leave 'presenteeism' unchecked? Are outside activities encouraged among employees: sports days, trips etc? Have you noticed if your staff socialise outside/after work with each other? If not, why not? Have you noticed if the workers ever socialise outside/after work with their manager/management? If not, why not?

4. Record the findings

It is good practice to record the main findings from the risk assessment and to share the information with the employees and their representatives. It goes without saying that the Findings should be incorporated into **the Safety Statement** along with the measures undertaken and changes made to the workplace.

REMEMBER: This record should help monitor progress and provide a strong ground of defence in any personal injury/ dismissal claim ever taken against the employer about the stress levels in his or her workplace.

5. Review the assessment at appropriate intervals & check the impact of measures taken

The Assessment should be reviewed whenever significant changes happen in the organisation. This also should be done in consultation with employees. The impact of measures taken to reduce work-related stress should be checked.

Practical examples: employers beware! the head in the sand is no longer a defence

Two examples highlight the problems of employers posed by the accumulation of the above common law and health and safety principles.

'Presenteeism'

The **first example** of how these principles are now highly relevant is the concept of '*presenteeism*' in the workplace. This is the opposite of the more familiar term '*absenteeism*' whereby a business suffers unduly from employees failing to turn up for work. Presenteeism occurs where employees, for reasons of due (undue?) diligence, competition with each other and of enhancing promotion prospects, remain significantly longer at the workplace than they have to in order to boost their productivity or output. They may do so without being required to by an employer. It is particularly common in large organisations with defined hierarchies.

'Biting off more than he can chew'

The **second example** is similar. This is where employees unilaterally take on more work or responsibility than they are required to do or than is necessary for the fulfilment of their lawfully allocated employment duties. This does not necessarily mean that they spend longer in the workplace but that they '*cram in more*'. Again, they may do so without being asked by their employer. They may suddenly find themselves out of their depth, unable to cope and unwilling or afraid to admit it.

A warning

Employers now beware! As well as the more normal type of claims, into the future, these are conditions of work for which liability may also attach to an employer and damages awarded. Depending on the size of the business and its levels of productivity, an employer should not leave an employee to his own devices when it comes to his workload, as, although most employees can be assumed to keep their workloads within reasonable limits, this assumption may not be guaranteed in all cases.

One important instance is if an employee has valid reasons to believe or the employer encourages a belief that the only way to get feedback and reward for efforts made, with a view to promotion, is to work longer or take on more responsibility than necessary. This creates role conflict and ambiguity and may serve to create hostility among employees in the course of their employment.

If such a system is imposed formally, encouraged informally or simply left unchecked, an employee, injured as a result of being overwhelmed by the stress of failing to cope with an ill-defined workload, may claim that these were conditions of work of which his employer was aware or ought to have been aware and which he should have taken steps to prevent.

Similarly, an employer is now likely to be exposed to an award of damages if a court concludes that he deliberately used or there was a deliberate use by others of occupational stress as a tool or a device to promote productivity and his employee consequently suffers a mental injury or illness as a result.

- Does an employer bully his or her employees to meet deadlines or targets?
- Does he or she use harassment to meet those deadlines or targets?
- Does he or she use aggression, threats, humiliation, abusive behaviour or language in order to achieve desired aims?
- Does he or she allow his or her managers or employees to do so and to inflict this treatment on others?
- Is he or she unaware that such tactics are being used when he or she ought to have been aware?
- Has he or she left such tactics unchecked?

Spotting the signs of stress: how to respond?

As a result, even with all the precautions outlined above, employers, line managers, supervisors and HR should still remain vigilant for the effects of work-related stress illnesses among the workforce. In particular, if an employer knows or suspects that an employee is either exposing himself or is exposed for some other reason (through bullying or harassment etc.) to harmful levels of work-related stress, then the employer must now act.

The intervention: one example

When deciding to intervene, if possible, and as most employers will appreciate, the non-confrontational or non-legalistic approach is always the most appropriate in this type of situation.

The chat

It may be useful to simply have an informal chat privately and confidentially with the employee enquiring as to the reasons for any ill health or erratic behaviour that is noticed. Prolonged or intermittent and regular absences from work are good examples of such problems. In the event that an employer is not in a position to spot the signs directly, it is also important to have a structure in place to allow *an employee to come forward* himself informally and to speak to another designated employee or supervisor confidentially. Furthermore, employers or their line managers and supervisors should have the systems in place to monitor any possible instances of stress-related injuries or their symptoms. This is what the courts and tribunals mean when they talk about what an employer *ought to have known* when awarding civil damages or compensation.

This is vital as, sometimes, employees are reluctant to admit to, or are even in denial of, a difficulty. This may also be the case in situations where the source of the stress is serious bullying or harassment. Many employees may not want to admit to a weakness or it may be that the bullying behaviour or harassment is associated with threats of violence.

By way of a general guide, this informal conversation approach usually includes a selection of some or all of the following points.[25] It should be held in a non-judgmental manner and tone. It should also be expressed that the matter is being raised solely out of concerns for the best interests of the employee and in order to discuss his or her options about how best to alleviate any symptoms of work-related stress. It may be helpful in the course of this conversation to indicate to the employee the esteem with which he or she is held in the organisation and that his or her hard work is and will remain valued by his employer. However, his or her health is more valuable in the long-term both to himself and to his employer. It is also appropriate to remind him or her (if

---

[25] Employers should always get legal advice on the specific circumstances of his or her situation.

thought necessary) that the content of the conversation is strictly confidential.

The formal complaint

On some occasions, dealing with the symptoms of work-related stress may necessarily involve formality. This may be particularly important where bullying or harassment causes the risk of stress-induced injury. This is because for an employer, a line manager or an HR officer to satisfactorily alleviate the risk in the long-term, the anti-bullying/harassment procedure may have to be utilised and thereafter the disciplinary procedure, if necessary. As such, where the employee feels unable to deal with the problem informally, in such instances, he or she should be made aware and encouraged to put a complaint concerning the precise incidents and alleged sources of the bullying or harassment related stress in writing to the employer directly or through a line manager or supervisor. This is dealt with in detail in Chapter 5.

Reduce the workload, increase resources, punish wrongdoing

However, once the symptoms are spotted or otherwise brought to the attention of a business, the employer or the appropriate person within that business who is charged with dealing with the problem must carefully listen, consider what he or she is told about the working environment by the employee and ultimately make any necessary changes either in terms of resources, discipline or redistribution of labour. In particular, remedial medical advice or therapy should be provided and paid for by the employer where possible, both to ascertain a better diagnosis of the problem and a treatment for it. Pending the outcome of these precautionary measures, if the employee remains in the workplace, the employer must direct him or her to reduce his or her workload by not engaging in the excessive work-related activity that *gives rise to concerns* of the stress related illness or injury. However, it may also be necessary to remove the employee from the workplace altogether for a defined period (see below). Moreover, where harassment or bullying is involved, as part of dealing with the stress, arrangements may have to be made to remove the parties from each other until the matter is investigated formally or otherwise informally resolved.[26]

Any permanent redefining of an employee's role and job specification should always be carried with his or her participation and cooperation as much as possible. However, ultimately, the redefinition of any roles should reflect and be supported by a clinical medical or psychiatric opinion obtained about the particular employee. Moreover, where bullying or harassment has occurred, certain employees may have to be permanently kept apart in the workplace. However, the role of an employer in this process is not an absolute one. He or she only has to take what are reasonable and proper steps in the particular circumstances of the business. In the event of any dispute or disagreement between the employer and the employee, this will prove important. An employee is not entitled to refuse out of hand to engage in this process or to reject any reasonable options put to him in good faith on the basis that he simply does not agree with them or that they are inconvenient to his established domestic or lifestyle arrangements. In the latter case, he will have to show that he attempted to re-arrange his domestic situation.[27]

This is a very sensitive issue and should be handled with the utmost caution. Any suggestion that an alteration to the terms or conditions of a worker's employment is motivated by reasons other than for the well being of that worker is

---

[26] See Chapter 5.

[27] *Reyes v. Print and Display Limited* [1999] E.L.R. 224 (EAT).

likely to be viewed by him or her as a pretext for demotion or humiliation and may lead to litigation.

Investigation and suspension

If the employer has a concern about a continuing, serious risk to the mental health of an employee which is work-related, it may be advisable that the employee be relieved of his or her duties for a period **on full salary** pending the employer investigating the matter and so that the advice and assistance of health or occupational professionals about what to do can be obtained.

In 1999, an Irish court expressly decided that this approach was acceptable.[28] A suspension on full pay must only last as long as it takes the employer to undertake this process and receive advice. In order to return to work, the employee should agree to abide by that advice and his failure to do so will not rebound on his employer. This approach is lawful in all cases where an employer suspects his employee is vulnerable to stress-related injury. This is an appropriate way of an employer living up to his duty of care.

Under no circumstances should this form of suspension ever be used as a disciplinary process for whatever reason.

Ultimately, where an employee is so ill, he or she may not be able to return to the workplace or it may not be safe to allow them to do so. In that case, it will be necessary for a more prolonged period of leave of absence in accordance with the contractual sick pay scheme where there is one.

Dismissing an employee suffering a work-related stress injury

On the one hand, such a dismissal may, *in principle*, be upheld if an employee is no longer capable by reason of long-term

[28] *Nolan v. Ryan Hotels* [1999] E.L.R. 214.

ill health to perform the job for which he or she was employed. In these circumstances, there is no legal duty on an employee to make 'light work' for an employee and an employee, after been accorded fair procedures, may be dismissed. However, *in practice*, for the employer who wishes to avoid litigation, this approach is increasingly loaded with difficulties, particularly when an employee is absent on sick leave and is furnishing medical certificates in the appropriate manner.

This is especially so where work-related stress is involved. In that situation, the employer's first response must always be to deal with the cause of the illness and to improve the working conditions of the ill employee rather than simply leave him languishing on sick leave. Only when this is done, taking account of the general suggestions above, should an employer even consider entering the realm of dismissal.

There are three possible consequences of a dismissal for work-related stress to bear in mind. Firstly, if the dismissal is not handled fairly, the employer is subject to the substantial statutory compensation regime for unfair dismissal. This is always on top of any damages for a personal injury claim that may be pursued in parallel through the civil courts. [29]

Secondly, a dispute of this nature may also lead to an injunction application being taken against an employer to restrain the dismissal. In particular, the High Court has been willing to look at the merits of such applications in recent years, particularly at the interlocutory stage, and, where just and equitable to do so, restrain purported wrongful dismissals by maintaining the terms and conditions of employment (up to and including full remuneration) pending the trial of the main action.[30] At the trial, an employee may be awarded

[29] In *Hyland v. Bestfood Services Ltd.*, UD 485/99. In this determination of the Employment Appeals Tribunal, £26,650 was awarded to the applicant when she was dismissed whilst on sick leave due to the medically certified risk of a heart attack provoked by work-related stress.

[30] *Rooney v. Kilkenny* [2001] E.L.R. *per* Kinlen J.

civil damages for wrongful dismissal on the basis of the loss suffered. This is also on top of any damages for personal injury.

Finally, in the context of work-related stress injuries, even if an employee does not wish to challenge a dismissal claim on the basis of ill health, for whatever reason, it is most likely that a personal injury action may, nevertheless, emerge. The dismissed employee will seek damages and allege that *the employer has either caused or failed to prevent that stress that caused the illness*. Indeed, the *Walker* case above is a perfect example of such a scenario.

As a result, quite apart from the need to secure medical advice in dealing with the stress-related symptoms of employees *remaining in* the workplace or only *temporarily removed* as a precaution, once an employer takes that further fateful decision to dismiss an employee who is on leave of absence and who is *unable to return* to work as a result of work-related stress, he must make *twice as sure* that he has obtained the necessary and appropriate professional advice, both legal and medical. With particular regard to all those vital warnings, before dismissing, an employer must, in particular, satisfy him/herself that he/she can show the following.

- Ill health is the reason for the dismissal;
- It is the substantial reason;
- The employee received fair notice that the question of his dismissal for incapacity was being considered;
- The employee was afforded the opportunity and means to respond and to challenge the decision.[31]

The employee must also have been *out of work for an*

[31] *Bolger v. Showerings (Ireland) Ltd* [1990] E.L.R. 184 *per* Lardner J.

unreasonable length of time and still cannot give a reasonable return date. What is 'reasonable' will depend on the specific circumstances of each case. However, important factors are the size and resources of a business, the opportunities to redistribute the workload, the importance of a position and the feasibility of getting a temporary replacement, the general effect on output and sales (particularly for small businesses) and an employee's past or likely future service with the business.

Unreasonable absences may also occur where the employee is out sick due to work-related stress on *an intermittent, although frequent, basis*. This is a prime example of where an employer should be on his or her guard to inquire as to any possible connection between the occurrence of such absences and symptoms of work-related stress. In this specific situation, where an employer suspects a problem of this nature but has not been furnished with any medical certificates by the employee, he or she or the appropriate designated person should discuss these absences with the employee. Where the problem is one that might benefit from medical assistance or opinion, the employee must be recommended to visit his or her doctor. An employer might also consider asking an employee to provide medical certificates for all such future absences, at the expense of the employer. This may be enough to resolve matters. However, where a problem does emerge, the employer must act accordingly as outlined above. Moreover, where the problem is medically certified as work-related stress, it is entirely inappropriate to view these absences as a disciplinary issue.

Ultimately, in the event that the situation does not improve and an employer decides that it has become reasonable to dismiss an employee for long-term ill health, he or she must afford an employee all fair procedures, any counselling or medical services available and warnings before doing so. This is an area where **extreme caution** is advised. Fair procedures are discussed in more detail in Chapter 5.

In practice, considerations about fairness may be implemented by the following means:[32]

- An employer must carry out all necessary enquiries to ascertain the likelihood of a reasonable return date. Discuss with an employee his or her current state of health and the likelihood of a return within a reasonable period. What is reasonable may again depend on factors outlined earlier and also other factors such as the size of the business and its resources.
- Obtain the agreement of the employee that the employer may arrange to obtain a medical opinion from a doctor about the likelihood of a return to work within a reasonable period.
- If the employee's doctor is unwilling or unable to give a prognosis on a return to work, ask the employee if he is prepared to submit to an examination by a third party. Unless the contract of employment makes provision for examination by a third party, the employee may refuse to do so and not be in breach. However, such a refusal is always susceptible to being found unreasonable by a court or tribunal and in such circumstances, the absence of a third party examination may not, in principle, negative the fairness of any subsequent dismissal.[33]
- If a medical opinion is obtained and it is still clear that an employee is unable to return to work, he or she should be visited again and the steps that the business is proposing to take discussed with him or her.
- If matters do not improve and, having duly considered the discussions with the employee including any suggestions

---

[32] Barry, O'Mara and Hayes, *Termination and Redundancy, A Guide To Implementing the Legislation* Dublin, (Round Hall Professional Publishing, 2002), pp.36 and 37.

[33] *Reyes v. Print and Display Limited* [1999] E.L.R. 224 (EAT).

or proposals, termination may be effected with full and proper notice to be given to the employee.

These steps incorporate the current procedure for dealing with ill health dismissals generally in Ireland. However, a recent decision, with particularly serious implications for employers in terms of their financial exposure for occupational stress injuries, has determined that the issue as to whether an employer has caused the stress in the first place is now directly relevant in determining both the *fairness* of any dismissal and also the amount of compensation that ought to be awarded in *compensation*. Therefore, the extent to which an employer may be able to protect him or herself against a successful legal claim to such dismissals is increasingly uncertain.

Edwards v. Governors of Hanson School. **Fairness and dismissals for work-related stress: a case of whistling past the graveyard?** [34]

Background

The applicant began working as a teacher with the respondent in 1993. From September 1996, he was off work by reason of depression caused by stress at work. He attributed his illness to years of unfair treatment at the hands of the school's headmaster, a Mr Chaplin. The applicant returned to work in March 1997 but by then the headmaster had decided that his attendance record should be treated as a disciplinary matter. At a disciplinary meeting on the 21st March 1997, the applicant was given a verbal warning that was to remain in force for six months. The applicant was off sick the following day, returned to work for two days in April and never returned to work again. After consulting the educational services'

[34] [2001] I.R.L.R. 733 (November).

occupational physician, who expressed the opinion that he would not be fit to return even to part-time work in the foreseeable future, the respondent decided that the applicant should be dismissed.

Judgment

Fairness: The decision rejected the proposition that an employer's treatment of an employee causing ill-health, which in turn causes incapability which the employer treats as a reason for dismissal, can never *of itself* make the dismissal unfair. In particular, Mr Justice Bell of the English Employment Appeals Tribunal (EAT) held that if the employer or someone for whom it is responsible has acted maliciously, or has wilfully caused an employee incapacitating ill-health, there is no reason why dismissal, *however fair the ultimate procedures in themselves*, should not lead to a finding of unfair dismissal. However, the EAT did not ultimately have to deal with that point in this case as the dismissal was unfair anyway due to lack of consultation by the employer.

Compensation: On this important issue, the law does not require that questions as to responsibility for the illness, making dismissal inevitable, must be ignored when deciding whether or not it is just and equitable to make a compensatory award for unfair dismissal. The words 'just and equitable' enable an employment tribunal to take full account of the conduct of the employer and the employee, provided that the award remains compensation of the employee rather than punishment of the employer. If it was found that misconduct for which the employers were liable caused or contributed to the applicant's ill health leading to his dismissal, it would be for the tribunal to assess whether it would be just and equitable that a compensatory award should follow and, if so, to what extent.

This decision has particular significance for stress-related injuries caused by workplace bullying or harassment. Indeed, the Irish EAT appears to have already begun the progression down this road.[35]

Are all the rights one-way? Factors that help an employer

It must be remembered that while health and safety practice aims to minimise stress from the workplace to the greatest extent possible, the law has a more limited aim.

Hard work and occupational stress within reasonable thresholds, although undesirable from a health and safety perspective, are still not prohibited by the common law.

No 'work to rule' charter: the common law and the workplace

Firstly, this is not a 'work to rule' charter or a 'straight-jacket' on the workplace. To satisfy the common law, an employee's work need only be cut back to the extent that he is no longer exposed to a risk of stress related injury to his health. However, there are two important *caveats* to this.

(i) A particular employee must always be competent to perform the work he undertakes and that he remains so by keeping it within safe parameters.

(ii) Many employees are limited already in the hours and under the conditions they can work by legislation anyway.

Moreover, as discussed above, to satisfy good health and safety practice, the aim should be rather more ambitious. A progressive approach to health and safety is often persuasive

---

[35] See Chapter 3: *Allen v. Independent Newspapers (Ireland) Limited*, UD 641/2000.

and one factor to which courts have regard. Moreover, promoting positive quality of life issues has a positive impact on the morale and loyalty of employees to their employer.

Contributory negligence

Secondly, it is open to an employer at law to argue that the employee contributed to his own injury and this argument may even succeed in many cases. However, contributory negligence is not a full defence for an employer to personal injury actions and this defence goes only to the amount of damages ultimately awarded to an employee.

Normally, a specific proportion of '*contribution*' will be arrived at by the judge and this proportion will then be deducted from the quantum of damages to which an employee would otherwise have been entitled.

If the precautions have not already been taken and the systems put in place, it is too late to try to escape liability by relying on the contribution of an employee to his own fate. Contributory negligence is likely to be found where:

(a) The employee adopts the working conditions that expose him or her to the risk of mental damage that has resulted in an injury in circumstances where the employer did not know or ought not to have known of this conduct;

The employee also owes his or her employer a duty of care not to expose himself or herself to a risk of injury of which he or she knew or ought to have known.

(b) The employee may be exposed to a stress-related mental injury but he does not complain to the employer either informally by talking to the employer or to a manager/ supervisor or formally by invoking a grievance procedure (if one is available).

However, this never acquits an employer from upholding his own duty to take reasonable steps to protect his employees.

An employer must always act as a reasonable and prudent employer would and this duty is independent of any duty of an employee to take reasonable steps to protect and to not expose himself to risks of work related injury. Contributory negligence is very unlikely to attach where:

(a) The employee does complain about a particular workplace practice or condition that may reasonably be expected to expose him to a risk of mental injury but the employer does not do anything about it or leaves a practice unchecked.

For example, when an employer, who receives a complaint, fails to take action against bullying or harassment targeted at an employee because he considers it merely to be workplace 'banter' or 'horseplay'. If the employee has to work alongside the bully in the course of his employment with the result that the work-related stress results in a personal injury, it will be no defence for an employer to argue that the employee contributed to his own injury by failing to keep his distance from the bully. Bullying is discussed in Chapter 3.

The 'Egg-Shell Skull' Rule

General overview

There is also in common law what is called the 'egg-shell skull' rule. This basically means that a defendant must take a plaintiff as he finds him. In other words, if the plaintiff suffers a serious injury in circumstances where most other individuals would suffer no injury or only minor injury then the defendant is not entitled to rely on this in order to seek to limit the award of damages to an amount appropriate for the minor injury only. Once the defendant foresees the particular type of injury to the plaintiff, he is liable for all the consequences of that injury that follow by reason of the plaintiff's particular vulnerability.

The core principle

For the employer, this means that, once the employee can surmount the various hurdles in proving that his employer reasonably foresaw a risk to his mental or psychiatric health brought on by work-related stress, by harassment or by bullying, then he will be liable for the full extent of that injury to the employee even if the stress and the related bullying or harassment was 'mild' on the scale of things.

Tailoring employer liability: One size does not fit all!

Furthermore, in any workforce, there may be a variety of personality types and dispositions, each of which may have different ways of dealing and coping with any negative experiences and hostilities they encounter in the workplace. Employees may also have different thresholds of resilience before which their health may start to suffer. Some employees are able to sustain a higher, more pressurised workload than others.

Therefore, employees are not expected to have a common or uniform reaction to similar work related stresses or hostilities. In particular, as we saw in *Cross*, this includes a multitude of symptoms up to and including the risk of suicide. In that case, it was specifically confirmed that:

> "If it had been proved that the worsening of the depression was caused by wrongful acts or omissions on the part of the [employer], and, that it was the worsening of his depression that led him to commit suicide, the [plaintiff] would, in

> my opinion, have been entitled to recover damages in respect of his death, notwithstanding the fact that his suicide was not proved to be reasonably foreseeable as a likely result of the wrongful acts or omissions. The ['Egg-Shell Skull'] rule cannot...be avoided by arguing that suicide by gunshot is a different kind of harm from depressive illness, when there is clear evidence that depressive illness greatly increases the likelihood of suicide."[36]

This is of particular importance to sensitive or mild mannered employees or other groups that may be particularly vulnerable such as junior or new members of staff or employees who may have a psychiatric history that makes them more prone to a recurrence of mental injury. In such cases, even mild bullying or harassment may have more serious consequences. This will result in a higher award of damages to such an employee. Of course, the plaintiff employee will still have to prove that he or she was exposed to a risk of mental injury that was *materially higher* than that which would ordinarily have affected a person in his or her position whether due to a vulnerability or to the unreasonable stresses of the conditions of work.

In short, being sensitive or mild mannered does not, in itself, prove the employee's case but it may result in higher damages for him if he does.

Vicarious Liability

General overview

On many occasions, an employer may not be the individual

---

[36] [2001] I.R.L.R. 336 at 364.

responsible for the wrongdoing about which an employee complains. Indeed, it is often the case that the employer may not even have been aware of the initial circumstances that has resulted in the claim against him. This is particularly the case where the wrongdoing complained of comprises of an act or omission that was not authorised by the employer but is carried out on the initiative of the claimant's fellow employees.

In these circumstances, an employer may still be held responsible for the stress, bullying or harassment suffered by the claimant employee on the basis that he is *vicariously liable* for the actions of his employees. This is of significant practical benefit to a claimant in a personal injury action since the employer, as the business owner, will be a better financial target from which to recover damages and court costs in the event that the claimant is successful. Indeed, in recent years, vicarious liability has even been described as a litigation 'loss distribution device'.

Are you your brother's keeper?

In simple terms, the answer to this question is *yes*. As such, vicarious liability is simply the means by which the law ensures that an employer remains responsible for the acts and omissions of his employees *carried out in the course of employment and within the scope of employment generally*.

In the context of employment law, the three ways in which an employer may be liable for the acts of his employees are:

1. Statute.
2. Breach of a common law duty of care to provide competent employees.
3. The common law rules on vicarious liability.

Statute

Where a piece of legislation expressly provides that an

employer is to be responsible for the acts, omissions or conduct of his employees then that creates an absolute duty for an employer. This is known as '*strict liability*'. In sexual harassment and harassment claims, if they are proved, then legislation provides that the employer is strictly liable where another employee has carried out the wrongful act.[37]

Competent employees

An employer is also liable at common law for the acts or omissions of employees in his workplace who are simply not up to the job. This is not vicarious liability in the real sense. This is because the doctrine of vicarious liability involves the transfer of one person's *negligence* to another for some reason. In order for an employee to be negligent he must have *failed to use* all the reasonable skill and care that he had in doing his work. However, in some cases an employee did *not have any* appropriate skill and care at all and cannot be said to have failed to use it in this way. Therefore, to ensure that an employer remained liable for an incompetent as well as a negligent employee, a specific duty of care was created.

Common law vicarious liability

At common law, an employer may be vicariously liable in Ireland:

- Where the wrongful acts themselves are authorised by the employer; or
- Where the act used by an employee is a wrongful and unauthorised mode of doing some authorised, lawful act of the employer; or

---

[37] Section 15 of the Employment Equality Act 1998. See Chapter 4 in detail.

- Where the wrongful acts complained of have not been authorised by the employer at all but are so connected with another act that he has authorised that they may be considered to be merely the mode of doing it.

Therefore, for employers this means the following:

Wrongful and authorised acts: Reaping what you sow?
As far as any wrongful acts authorised by an employer are concerned, the situation is quite straight-forward and he or she will be held to account for those acts.

Wrongful modes of doing lawful, authorised acts: the ends justify the means?
Similarly, if some mode or method is used to achieve some authorised, lawful end desired and set by an employer, then the employer will also be deemed responsible for any wrongful conduct arising out of the efforts to meet such ends. Employers must always bear in mind that the ends never justify unlawful means.

An example might be where a foreman or manager subjects employees under his control to bullying, harassment or unsafe levels of work in order to meet certain deadlines or targets set by the employer.

'So Connected': An opt-out or a catch-all rule?
However, an employer's exposure to liability for the conduct of his employees also depends on the meaning given to the term '*so connected*' and this has been treated differently over the years. It may nowadays include activities and conduct that many employers may find surprising, if not alarming.

A Health Board v. B.C. and the Labour Court: Sex assault of a health board worker[38]

In this Irish case, the claimant was a female health board worker who had been sexually assaulted by two male employees of that Health Board in the workplace. The claimant argued that the Health Board should be held legally responsible for the actions of the two male employees. It was accepted in the High Court that an employer could be held vicariously liable when his employee was acting negligently or *even criminally*. However, the nature and scope of the employment would be an important issue in any such decision. As such, the court concluded that it could not envisage any employment in which an employee would be engaged in which a sexual assault could be regarded as so connected with it as to amount to an act within its scope.

Lister and Others v. Hesley Hall Ltd: Child abuse at an English boarding school[39]

The background

However, in this recent English House of Lords' case, it has indeed been held that such acts by an employee can result in an employer being held liable. This case involved repeated acts of sexual abuse of young school children by a school warden at the Defendant school for maladjusted and special needs pupils. The plaintiffs brought a personal injury for damages against the school on the basis that it was liable for the actions of the warden, its employee. On the basis of the conventional approach, the lower courts had held in this case that the conduct fell outside the scope of employment because the indecent assault was not an unauthorised mode of doing

---

[38] [1994] ELR 27.
[39] [2001] I.R.L.R. 472 (July).

some act authorised by the employers but was instead an independent act outside the course of employment.

The judgment

However, the Law Lords, in their judgment, described both as transforming and redefining the law, held in favour of the plaintiffs.

It was held that the correct approach was to concentrate on the relative closeness of the connection between the nature of the employment and the wrongdoing complained of.

Is the employee's conduct so closely connected with his employment that it would be fair and just to hold the employer vicariously liable?

Fair and just

Here, the sexual abuse was inextricably linked with the carrying out by the warden of his duties. The sexual assaults were carried out in the employer's time and on the premises while the warden was supposed to be also busy caring for the children. The warden had abused the position accorded to him through his employment in the school. The employee's position as warden and the resulting close contact with the pupils which that work involved created a sufficiently close connection between the acts of abuse committed and the work which he had been employed to do. Therefore, it would be **fair and just** to hold the defendant employer variously liable for injury and damage sustained and the court so held.

Two approaches: One conclusion?

It is clear that the scope of what constitutes vicarious liability is expanding. All employers must be aware of this into the future. This is clear from the decision in *Lister*. As such, the difference now between the traditional Irish common law approach and the new English case is a very striking one.

The implied authority test: Play it by the book?

On the one hand, in Ireland, in deciding what acts of an employee should or could fall within the scope of his employment, there must be some basis for finding that the act or improper mode is **one capable of being authorised by or derived from the authority of, even if implicitly or indirectly**, the employer. In doing so, the purpose or object of the employment relationship entered into will be examined to see if any act or mode of acting of a negligent or criminal employee is referable back to some purpose or objective as a justification.

However, where an employer neither knows of nor authorised the wrongful conduct, the plaintiff employee must prove that the wrongful acts or wrongful modes of doing an act fell within some general purpose or objective of the employment duties.

In turn, it is open to the employer to argue that since the wrongful acts are neither so close to any act authorised by him nor to any modes of acting in pursuit of that authorised act under the employment relationship, then it could never be required of an employee in the course of his employment.

Conclusion

Since the act of sexual assault was so outside what was required of an employee in his employment then it could never be considered one of the objects or purposes of an employment relationship. As such, it does not fall within the scope of any act or mode of acting that could ever be authorised, even implicitly, as necessary to fulfil an objective or purpose in the course of employment and, therefore, does not fall within the scope of that employment. Therefore, an employer could only be found liable if one or a group of employees, on their own initiative, inflicted injury or illness through the bullying, harassment of another worker where it was done to fulfil an objective or purpose of employment.

Example: A manager bullying employees to meet work targets or deadlines.

The 'nature of the job' test: Check the small print!

On the other hand, in England, as a result of *Lister*, it appears that this view is now entirely reversed.

The conduct

The vital test in attaching vicarious liability is now provided in the following questions posed:

> **Can the wrongful conduct be attributed to the relative closeness between the nature of the work in which an employee is engaged and his wrongdoing?**
>
> **If so, is it just and fair to hold the employer liable?**

Under this approach, the characteristics of the job such as its responsibilities, functions and privileges (as distinct from only its purpose or object) should be looked at in order to identify if they are capable of leading or contributing to the conduct complained of.

If so, what precautions and preventative measures were put in place to prevent workplace responsibilities, functions or privileges being abused through the committing of these acts or this conduct?

In this case, the authority of an employer is irrelevant, since it may be accepted that the wrongful act is one that could or would never have been authorised by an employer even implicitly but instead is an abuse associated with or arising out of some characteristic or function of the work for which a worker is employed.

Conclusion

Since the employee's position as warden, and the resulting close contact, control, trust and intimacy that the work involved, had the effect of creating a *sufficiently close connection between the acts of abuse committed and the nature of the work which he had been employed to do*, then it is fair and just to consider such acts to fall within the scope of his employment and as perpetrated in the course of his employment.

The risk of wrongdoing: an argument to bear in mind

One limitation that may have been placed on the general applicability of this rule is found in the following question posed by Lord Millett in his judgment in *Lister*:

> Could the employer's objectives have been achieved without *a serious risk* of the employee committing that kind of wrong?

His Lordship considered that serious risks of wrongdoing are those that **experience shows are inherent in the nature of the business**. If this is shown and the wrong has in fact been committed, only then ought the employer be liable for it. The fact that his employment gave an employee *the opportunity* to commit the wrong is not enough to make his employer liable. This provides some protection to an employer and holds back the floodgates somewhat.

Firstly, it means that there must be some fundamental attributes of the business that gave rise to the serious risk. It may be that there is a particular structure necessary to run a particular type of business or that the type of employment it provides is one that, if abused, is responsible for the wrong committed. Four likely examples would be **power, trust, absence of regular scrutiny** and **secrecy** and the risks of workplace bullying, harassment, violence or abuse that they create and cause.

Secondly, it means that the experiences of the employer, those of colleagues in the same type of business and the information available to him from professional bodies about the job must show him that it causes a risk of wrongdoing and has in fact resulted in that particular type of wrongdoing in the past. In light of all the publicity and information aimed at employers and the amount of bullying and harassment cases being exposed in the workplace, nowadays, it could scarcely be argued by an employer that there was no general experience, or, that he had no experience showing him, of a serious risk that employees commit acts of bullying and harassment by abusing their positions in the course of employment.

An example that might help to explain what such an inherent risk might mean in the context of bullying or harassment related stress is found in the following recent passage from the EAT:

> "Human beings by their nature have a propensity to be cruel. This propensity has the potential to be realised in an environment where a firm strong-minded individual is in charge of a person of weaker character. When factors such as dislikes, demands and assertions of power enter into the equation, a type of harassment on a minor scale can arise, and, if this left unattended to, it is likely to fester to full scale bullying or harassment."[40]

However, the High Court and Supreme Court in Ireland must pronounce on their view of *Lister* before a definitive view can be concluded as to vicarious liability at common law for

---

[40] *Browne v. Ventelo Limited,* UD 597/2001, July 16, 2002.

cases of serious workplace misconduct such as bullying or harassment and any consequent stress-related injury they cause.

The Future: Vigilance is the Key

Therefore, for employers, in the coming years, it must be remembered that **vigilance with regard to workplace behaviour is the key** to minimising exposure to allegations of vicarious liability. The precise scope and effect of this decision on the common law will be more fully worked out by later cases. As a result, this is an area on which employers, managers, trade unions, HR personnel, insurers and their legal advisers must keep a keen eye, into the near future, as it is an issue of key importance to the distribution of legal liability in bullying and harassment claims.

Post '*Lister*' in Ireland: A new varnish or a blank canvass?

Two matters have a bearing on this question.

> **Firstly**, *Lister* relates not to injured employees but to children at a boarding school. On that basis, a difference may be made between it and other decisions on occupational injury. However, it is clear that it was based on the nature of the employment relationship between the warden and the defendant school and from that perspective it has an important application to employment law also.
>
> **Secondly**, *Lister* is not applicable in Ireland, although, it is a highly persuasive one for Irish courts because it is from the House of Lords. Moreover, the trend in recent years has been a distinct willingness in Irish

courts to have regard to the reasoning of earlier English decisions in the employment law area.

As a perfect example of these legal developments in Ireland, it has been held in a determination of the statutory employment tribunal (the Employment Appeals Tribunal, discussed in the next chapter) in 2002 that bullying, harassment, intimidation and sexual harassment of an employee may be the responsibility of an employer for allowing or permitting such activity to occur within the employment relationship. This is on the basis that the employer ought to have reasonably foreseen or ought to have been aware of this anti-employment behaviour. Importantly, it was stated that the failure to compile an adequate Safety Statement may be enough now to support such a view.[41]

What is certain is that more wrongful acts of employees will be deemed in the future to fall within the scope of their employment, even if committed without any authority of the employer whether express or implied (no matter how tenuously!). However, the burden to be discharged by a plaintiff employee will remain a significant one.

Under *Lister*, it must be fair and just to hold an employer liable and the wrong, most likely, must not be opportunistic.

In Conclusion: What to Look Out For?

In conclusion, therefore, in both small and larger workforces and workplaces, there is now a greater onus than ever before on employers to have structures, guidelines and policies in place, at all levels of the workforce, to ensure that the employees conduct themselves responsibly and are aware of the importance of complying with the guidelines and policies

[41] *Browne v. Ventelo Limited,* UD 597/2001, July 16, 2002.

provided for them by their employer.

Moreover, employers should now have regard to the nature or characteristics of particular jobs and positions within a business or organisation in order to identify the seriousness and likelihood of any risks that they pose to employees.

This is particularly important at the managerial level where the risks of power and authority being abused or being arbitrarily applied to more junior employees through bullying, harassment or inordinately heavy workloads are greatest. In many cases, this is done to pursue particular business objectives such as meeting targets or deadlines.

In the future, in light of their developing and increasingly sophisticated attitude to work-related stress, the courts are also more likely to hold that a reasonable and prudent employer would have had an assessment in writing specifically of this risk along with the preventative anti-bullying and anti-harassment structure in place. Therefore, an employer who does so and implements it effectively may see the likelihood of his being found responsible for the bullying, harassment and the consequent claims thereof greatly diminished. This may be all the more the case in the event that the Irish courts move along the same path as their UK counterparts towards the view that bullying, harassment and their consequent stress-related effects are environmental risks that can be identified and prevented like any other.

Therefore, in the next chapter, the precise scope and specific requirements of anti-bullying policy and law will be provided. In Chapter 4, the anti-harassment laws will be outlined.

Chapter 3

Bullying in the Workplace: The Value and Price of Dignity

General Overview

So, what is all the fuss about?

In any human organisation, there is always a risk of bullying. This fact is nothing new to employers or indeed to their employees. Indeed, modern statistics seem to confirm the continuing pervasiveness of the problem. In 2001, the results of a survey across the entire European Union indicate that 9% of workers in Europe, or 12 million people, reported being bullied in the twelve-month period in 2000 alone.[1] Moreover, the prevention of workplace bullying is now one of the specific objectives of the European Commission in its new Health and Safety strategy.[2]

Therefore, what is new is the way in which bullying is treated and viewed nowadays. Unlike in the past, it is becoming less likely that an employer will escape liability on the basis either that he did not or could not have known of the occurrence of bullying or of the effect it was having on a particular employee. Many publications and guidelines have been aimed at employers in recent years specifically highlighting the need to deal with bullying as an unethical,

---

1 *Third European Survey on Work Conditions, 2000*. European Foundation for the Improvement of Living and Working Conditions, Luxembourg 2001.

2 Communication from the Commission-*Adapting To Change in Work and Society*: A New Community Strategy on Health and Safety at Work 2002-2006.

oppressive conduct, in itself, quite apart from the levels or nature of the injury to which it exposes an employee.

In short, an employee has a right not to be bullied at work. The employer has a duty to uphold that right.

This new approach culminated in 2001 in Ireland with the publication of the Report of the Task Force on The Prevention of Workplace Bullying: Dignity At Work, The Challenge of Workplace Bullying.[3] This involved a comprehensive, extensive and worthy study of workplace bullying. It recommended that a Code of Practice on Workplace Bullying be compiled for the purpose of providing an employer with best practice in the avoidance of bullying in his or her workplace.[4]

As of March 1, 2002, this Code of Practice has been in place and its terms, although not binding on the courts, are admissible in evidence against employers in criminal proceedings specifically. It is likely that they will also be very important in cases before the civil courts. As a result, employers must be mindful of it and the likelihood that it will be a persuasive factor in the attitude and approach of the courts to workplace bullying into the future.

A basic warning

Employers must now, therefore, be aware of the meaning of the term 'bullying in the workplace', how to identify it and what do about it. Bullying has been given a specific meaning and importance in the area of employment law in Ireland and it will be too late to play catch-up once proceedings arrive at the door.

On the other hand, those employers with an effectively

---

[3] Health and Safety Authority, Government Publications, Dublin, 2001.

[4] By virtue of a power of the Health and Safety Authority under s. 30 of Safety, Health and Welfare at Work Act 1989.

implemented anti-bullying policy to deal with complaints from the outset and in conformity with best practice are equally provided with a very strong defence to any litigation.

How to Identify The Hazards Of Bullying

The definition

There is no definition of bullying that is agreed upon internationally. In Ireland, the leading definition of work-related bullying now is that it is:

"**Repeated, inappropriate behaviour**, direct or indirect, whether verbal, physical or otherwise, conducted by one or more persons against another or others, at the place of work or in the course of employment, which could reasonably be regarded as undermining the individual's right to dignity at work. An **isolated incident of behaviour** described in this definition may be an affront to dignity at work but, as a once-off incident, is not considered to be bullying."[5]

Behaviour covered by the definition: Dignity under attack

Bullying is essentially any behaviour or conduct capable of undermining an employee's dignity. Two types of bullying situation may be identified:[6]

> Bullying as a consequence of an escalated inter-personal conflict;

---

5 Report of the Taskforce on the Prevention of Workplace Bullying, "*Dignity At Work: The Challenge of Workplace Bullying*", Health and Safety Authority, Dublin, Government Publications Office, 2001.

6 *FACTS*, European Agency For Safety and Health at Work, Fact Sheet No.23, Belgium, 2002.

> Bullying, where the victim has not been involved in a conflict, but is accidentally in a situation where the perpetrator exerts his or her acts of aggression and frustration on others. 'Scape-goating' is an example.

As such, there is a multitude of behaviour that comes within the grasp of what is considered bullying. Furthermore, social norms and attitudes change over time as do the types of behaviour expressing them. For example, the type of behaviour that may be acceptable to a younger workforce may not be acceptable to an older one or vice versa. Or similarly, if the workforce is either predominantly male or female.

This is not to make a judgment of any type or to make any arbitrary distinctions but it is only simply to remind employers that they should be in tune to what is appropriate behaviour among their particular workforce. A good example is the use of bad or coarse language among the workforce.

Upholding dignity: A full time job?

However, employers should not unduly worry that every little indiscretion or perceived slight of an employee will result in some form of compensation claim or an award of compensation against them. On the other hand, they should never be so complacent as to simply ignore complaints that they consider to be minor.

Therefore, in the first instance, bullying must be distinguished from **inter-personal conflicts** that, although undesirable, are not necessarily considered as bullying in a legal sense.[7] Bullying, by its definition, is something more than an inter-personal conflict. Such conflicts may be distinguished from bullying because they do not result in the

---

7 *FACTS*, European Agency For Safety and Health at Work, Fact Sheet No.23, Belgium, 2002.

dignity of one party being undermined. This may be because it is an interaction with which they can cope and adequately react to. Such conflicts may arise from many sources such as professional disagreements or competitive tensions between workers. However, bullying is conduct that, because it is so intentionally hostile to and abusive of primarily one party or one group to the transaction (whether because they are more junior, less powerful etc.), it is capable of undermining that worker's or group's dignity.

However, the scope of this distinction remains one that will have to be clarified in the civil courts and industrial relations tribunals over coming years.

Secondly, the prevention of bullying is not about ensuring good manners in the workplace (although it always helps!) but about outlawing repeated conduct that can *reasonably be regarded* as attacking and undermining dignity. Furthermore, once-off acts or events may not be considered in Ireland as behaviour manifesting bullying.

On the one hand, this means that a court or tribunal will look at the behaviour complained of and the definition of bullying above and consider if a normal, reasonable or ordinary employee would be offended or upset by it in the circumstances. If it cannot be reasonably regarded as bullying, then the claim will fail. On the other hand, it is also the case that behaviour that an employer did not consider to be bullying may now be held to be so.

For example, employers must be very careful from now on not to simply accept at face value or to take for granted that particular workplace behaviour is only 'banter', 'slagging' or 'horseplay'. It may, in fact, be reasonably regarded as manifesting bullying behaviour that should prompt an employer to act.

The banter and horseplay may not be going so far or have yet reached a stage as to impair the health of an employee but may nevertheless be conduct with which the bullied employee takes serious offence and finds intolerable. This conduct, if brought about or left unchecked by an employer, may lead to other **forms of litigation** such as an unfair/ wrongful dismissal claim in the event that a bullied employee resigns or a statutory claim of harassment (see below).

Moreover, at common law, an employer who knew or ought to have known of an employee's 'playful or vicious propensities' and has failed to take steps to prevent them from resulting in injury, whether physical or psychological, to another is deemed to have been responsible for the same. Also an employer, in the past, has been held liable in common law to workers injured by a confirmed and reckless practical joker.[8]

Do I have to wait for a complaint before I act?

Early action should always be taken against a destructive work environment. As with the issue of stress, an employer should not presume the absence of problems simply because there are no complaints. There may be circumstances where an employee will not make a complaint to his employer. Firstly, it may be because the employee feels afraid of the consequences of doing so or he may be in denial of a problem entirely. Secondly, the very agents of the bullying may be the senior management or the employer directly. Thirdly, the absence of a complaint may be as a result of the very non-existence of or deficiencies in the anti-bullying policy or procedures of the business. Fourthly, the employer has a duty of care to act independently of his employees. This covers not only cases where an employer is aware of a problem in his workplace environment but also where he ought to have been aware of it.

[8] *Waters v. MPC* [1997] I.C.R. 1073 and *Hudson v. Ridge Manufacturing Limited* [1957] 2 Q.B. 348. These decisions have more recently been cited with approval in Ireland in *Browne v. Ventelo Limited,* UD 597/2001, July 16, 2002.

Employers should not sit idly by and wait for employees to complain[9]

A three-pronged approach is always preferable in seeking to minimise legal exposure. Firstly, the employer should implement a general preventative system of workplace bullying. Secondly, he should undertake specific action on foot of complaints of bullying in the workplace. Thirdly, he should undertake improvements in the social work environment.

The workers and their representatives should be involved in this approach in order to be fully effective. In the event of an employer taking positive action to prevent bullying in his workplace in such a manner, it provides a strong defence in the event of any future claim against him or her, especially where the claimant employee has not complained and invoked the grievance procedure.

The behaviour to look out for

There are certain types of behaviour that may be identified as manifesting bullying behaviour. These inappropriate types of behaviour may:

- Humiliate;
- Intimidate;
- Verbally abuse;
- Physically abuse or threaten abuse;
- Use aggressive or obscene language;
- Make jokes that are offensive to one worker or to a group of workers whether by spoken word, e-mail or image.

---

9 *FACTS*, European Agency For Safety and Health at Work, Fact Sheet, No.23, Belgium 2002.

- Victimise;
- Exclude and isolate;
- Intrude through pestering, spying or stalking;
- Give repeated unreasonable assignments to duties that are obviously unfavourable to one individual;
- Give repeated impossible deadlines or impossible tasks;
- Imply threats;
- Attack a worker's reputation by rumour, gossip, innuendo or ridicule.

This list is non-exhaustive but gives an employer a good feel for the territory he or she is in. Of course, this behaviour may not only be that of the employer but also that of the managers or fellow employees of the victim.

Assessing the Risk

The inappropriate behaviour above indicates bullying when it is repeated and targeted at one employee or group of employees.

Circumstances associated with a higher risk of bullying

A number of factors associated with the workplace or with the conditions of work imposed there may expose an employee to a greater risk of bullying. It is important for employers when assessing the risks of bullying to be aware of what these circumstances are. They include:

Employment tenure

A bully may regard new, casual and temporary/contract staff

as easier targets than permanent, established colleagues. Insecure employment generally in a business is a factor increasing the likelihood of bullying in the workplace.

Size of the workforce/enterprise

It may be easier for bullying or the behaviour patterns that give rise to it to continue remain unchecked in a larger organisation. Moreover, the larger a business is, the greater the risks of work-related stress, role conflicts among employees and more onerous levels of work demands. These are also factors that increase the risk of bullying in the business.

Organisation culture

An employer or an organisation may condone bullying behaviour or fail to recognise it as a problem.

Organisational change in the workplace

Organisational change in the workplace can increase the risk of workplace bullying. These include:

- A new manager or supervisor;
- Change in ownership;
- Reorganisation of the company or business;
- The introduction of new technology.

Management of relationships in the workplace

Bullying is more likely to occur in workplaces lacking an effective human resource management system that supports work relationships among employees and promotes common workplace values and goals among employees. The risk of bullying may also be increased where there is a poor relationship between staff and management and a low level of satisfaction with leadership in the business.

Gender or age Imbalance

Bullying may be more likely to occur where there is a gender or age imbalance in the workforce.

Public interface

Employers must remember that the definition of bullying in Ireland relates to behaviour perpetrated in the workplace *or* in the course of employment. Furthermore, there is no requirement that the behaviour has to be conducted exclusively by the employer or employees but simply by 'persons.' Therefore, the customers, business associates or independent contractors of the employer are all covered by this definition so long as the bullying occurs in the workplace **or** in the course of employment. This also means that an employee may bring a claim for work-related bullying occurring outside of the workplace if it is, nevertheless, suffered in the course of employment such as training seminars, conferences or work-related social events.

Service industry beware!

Jobs dealing with the public in the services industry may be particularly prone to intimidatory or hostile conduct. This depends on the nature of the service being provided, the workloads involved, the location of the workplace and the attitudes of the clients receiving the service. An employee can now blame his own employer when he is bullied by members of the public in the workplace or in the course of his employment even if the employer and his other employees, although innocent of the actual acts complained of, leave their occurrence unchecked.

TAKING PRECAUTIONARY MEASURES

Introduce and implement an effective anti-bullying culture

Introduce a positive work environment

The preparation and implementation of an effective Anti-Bullying Culture is vital so as to encourage a more positive relationship between employees in the workplace and to make bullying an anti-social behaviour there. However, it also ensures that, should bullying occur, there are procedures in place, supported by management to deal with it. Anti-Bullying culture simply means developing a workplace environment with standards and values against bullying. This may comprise the following factors:

- An Awareness by all of what is bullying;
- An Investigation of the extent and nature of the problem;
- The Formulation of an **Anti-Bullying Policy**;
- The effective communication of workplace standards and values to all levels in the organisation through staff manuals, information meetings or newsletters.

Introduce an anti-bullying policy

It is vital to have an anti-bullying policy. In the preparation and implementation of an effective policy, similar considerations will apply in relation to consultation, participation and representation as in the case of a conventional Safety Statement.

The Health and Safety Authority of Ireland publication entitled 'Guidelines on Preparing Your Safety Statement And Carrying Out Risk Assessments' advises:

> "The law requires you to put in place a safety

> consultation programme that facilitates participation by all employees in health and safety matters. Participation by your employees supports your risk control by encouraging their 'ownership' of health and safety policies and procedures. It also gives them an understanding that your workplace and the people working in it benefit from good health and safety performance. Pooling knowledge and experience through the safety representative means that health and safety becomes everybody's business."[10]

This advice is equally relevant to an anti-bullying policy.

Training and instruction

Awareness, supervision and training

Employees should be provided with such information, instruction, training and supervision as is necessary to ensure the prevention of workplace bullying. This should include:

- Making employees aware of the Anti-Bullying Policy;
- Information on the Appropriate Behaviour to Comply with the Policy;
- Training, if needed, in order to comply with the policy;
- Assistance, if necessary, to overcome bullying, as well as adequate and informed supervision of the work environment;
- The Awareness-Raising of Managers, supervisors, and employees to deal with bullying complaints;

---

[10] *Code of Practice on the Prevention of Workplace Bullying* HSA, Dublin, March 2002.

- Improving management responsibility and competence in handing conflicts and communication;
- Establishing an independent contact for employees;
- Involving employees and their representatives in the risk assessment and prevention of bullying.

Job design

Another issue that may arise and may influence whether bullying may occur in a particular environment involves the nature of a person's position and role profile within the workplace. Precautions should be taken through job and work design. As a matter of good practice, employers should plan each worker's position and define his or her role as clearly as possible. They should be provided with the necessary resources, information and training to carry out their functions. These may include:

- A written description of main duties and responsibilities;
- A clear line of supervision;
- Giving each worker a reasonable choice on how to carry his or her work;
- Decreasing, as much as possible, the amount of monotonous and repetitive work;
- Increasing information about goals;
- Developing the leadership style;
- Avoiding unclear role and task specifications.

This should be reviewed in a collaborative manner on an on-going basis and changes in the job description or content should be communicated clearly to the individual **and** to those working alongside him or her. This assists in creating an environment where bullying is less likely to occur, as the role of each employee will be clear and transparent at all times both to the employee and his or her colleagues and to the managers/supervisors.

Each employee acknowledges his or her responsibility

Every employee is responsible to safeguard his own safety and welfare as well as that of his or her colleagues who may be affected by his acts or omissions while at work. At law, each employee owes his employer a duty of care not to expose himself or his fellow employees to a risk to their safety and health.

Therefore, each employee must be made aware of their duty not to place the safety and welfare of colleagues at risk by engaging in bullying or, when in a position of authority, to take the appropriate steps if or when it occurs. If not, the employer faces vicarious liability for failure.

The Consequences of Failure

Bullying claims, depending on circumstances, may be dealt with in either of three ways:

1. The Industrial Relations Route;
2. The Constructive Dismissal Route;
3. The Health and Safety Route.

1. The industrial relations route

The Rights Commissioner Service

This Service operates under the ambit of the Labour Relations Commission ('LRC'). Rights Commissioners are independent adjudicators appointed by the Minister for Enterprise and

Employment. They may investigate and make findings on any trade dispute referred to the Labour Relations Commission. A trade dispute is one between the employer and an employee about some aspect of the employee's terms and conditions of employment. Claims relating to bullying are included and these may be brought by individual or small groups of workers. The findings of a Rights Commissioner are issued to the parties in the form of non-binding recommendations. Either party has the right to appeal the recommendations to the Labour Court, which will then make a binding determination on the matter. Rights Commissioners deal with the vast majority of bullying cases referred to the LRC.[11]

The Labour Court

The general basis for any claim being brought to this Court must be that a trade dispute exists. The Court has always held the view that bullying in the workplace, affecting as it does an employee's conditions of employment, falls within the definition of a trade dispute. There are three ways in which a bullied employee can bring a claim to this court.

Firstly, the Labour Court has the power to hear appeals from a Rights Commissioner in relation to its recommendations about the bullying. The parties to the dispute are bound by the determination of the Court on appeal. However, it is not legally enforceable.[12]

Secondly, a worker involved in a trade dispute may request the Labour Court to investigate the dispute directly. The worker must agree to be bound by the determination.

---

[11] Section 13 of the Industrial Relations Act 1969; Report of the Taskforce on the Prevention of Workplace Bullying, "*Dignity At Work: The Challenge of Workplace Bullying*", Health and Safety Authority, Dublin, Government Publications Office, 2001.

[12] Section 13(9) of the Industrial Relations Act 1969.

However, once again, it is not a legally enforceable order against an employer. The vast majority of bullying cases taken to the Labour Court are dealt with in this way.[13]

Finally, where another branch of the LRC (apart from a Rights Commissioner) has investigated a dispute and is satisfied that no further efforts on its part will resolve matters, the parties in dispute may request that the Court take up the matter and make a determination. This determination is not legally enforceable.[14]

Saehan Media (Irl) Ltd v. A Worker. Work-related stress goes it alone[15]

This 1999 case is a very timely reminder of the new, vigorous approach to work-related stress now being taken by the industrial relations bodies. The employee was the head of security at the employer company. He alleged that, in the course of his employment, he was subjected to bullying, intimidation and harassment. As a result, he suffered the effects of work-related stress. He made a complaint through the appropriate procedure. However, the response of his employer was considered inadequate. A reference of the complaint was made directly to the Labour Court where an investigation was undertaken at the request of the parties. The Court determined that the incidents complained of did not, in themselves, constitute bullying. However, it accepted that the employee was, nevertheless, suffering from work-related stress. In doing so, it stated:

> "Work-related stress is recognised as a health and safety issue and employers have an obligation to

---

[13] Section 20(1) of the Industrial Relations Act 1969.
[14] Section 26(1) of the Industrial Relations Act 1990.
[15] [1999] E.L.R. 41.

> deal with instances of its occurrence which are brought to their attention."

Compensation in the sum of £500 was recommended. What is important in this case is not so much the amount of compensation but that compensation was awarded at all. The Labour Court essentially unshackled work-related stress from the constraints of the actual allegation of bullying and considered its presence as a wrong in itself separate to the issue of bullying. It must be borne in mind that the situation was made worse by the employer's failure to respond.

Nevertheless, this is a clear warning that the industrial tribunals are applying the higher standards of recommended health and safety practice (as outlined in this book in Chapter 2) rather than the more conservative common law approach. As such, employers are now financially exposed to stress claims simply for failing to deal with its cause and effects when they arise.

This surely now provides another strong incentive for employers to look wider than just to issues of negligence and contractual duties under common law when dealing with stress.

2. The constructive dismissal route

The basic idea

Where an employee has no option but to resign, with or without notice, as a result of bullying, a claim for either **wrongful** or **unfair** dismissal may be taken. Such a claim is likely to be taken in parallel with personal injury proceedings but not necessarily so. For example, an employee may have had to resign not because he or she had suffered a stress related illness but because he or she wished to avoid illness or injury in the first place. The latter situation is harder for the employee to prove. Nevertheless, the principle is the same even if the motivation is different.

A claim of constructive dismissal is not defeated where the employee does not give any reasons for her resignation or where the reasons given when challenging the dismissal are different to those given when the employee resigned. The law accepts that there may be important reasons why an employee may not want to record her actual intolerance of the workplace at the time she has to resign and that this should not automatically damage a claimant's credibility. The main reason may be that he/she is under a 'duress of circumstance'. This is where there are factors placing such an inordinate pressure on the will of an employee that she does not give the real reasons. One example is where the employee may fear a real detriment such as being refused a reference. Factors such as these may only become apparent at the conclusion of all the evidence at a hearing and therefore the courts and tribunal prefer to proceed rather than unfairly write off what might be a valid claim.[16]

The choice available

In the case of wrongful dismissal, the employee will rely on the terms of his or her contract of employment, whether express or implied by common law, and he or she will seek damages arising out of the dismissal in the civil courts as a breach of contract.

Alternatively, the employee may elect to take an unfair dismissal claim and seek to rely on his or her statutory entitlements by pursuing a claim under the Unfair Dismissals Acts 1977-1993 as a breach of statute. The 1977 Act expressly provides that a dismissal occurs when an employee has no

---

[16] See *Browne v. Ventelo Limited,* UD 507/2001, July 16, 2002. In that case, the claimant had filled out a form before she left recording her reasons for leaving as 'travelling.' This was held not to undermine her credibility in light of all the other circumstances of her case.

option but to terminate the contract of employment, with or without prior notice, because of the conduct of the employer. The claim is heard before either **a Rights Commissioner** or **the Employment Appeals Tribunal** ('EAT') and not in the civil courts. The EAT is an independent body bound to act judicially between the parties. An employee has to choose between either the wrongful claim or the unfair claim. He cannot take both.

Wrongful or unfair? The factors of choice

Whether an employee will proceed by wrongful or unfair dismissal will usually depend on his seniority, his professional status, and his period of service with an employer and the terms of his contract of employment (in particular the notice period to which an employee may be entitled on dismissal).

'Wrongful'

On the one hand, if an employee believes that the damages to which he is entitled at common law for breach of his contract are greater than the amount to which he would be entitled under statute, or if an employee is not yet entitled to a statutory claim, he or she will ordinarily pursue a wrongful dismissal claim. The claim will rely on the application and interpretation of the actual terms of the contract. Therefore, the choice whether to go down this path will invariably depend on the particular terms of employment contract.

For example, in constructive dismissal, where an employee resigns without giving notice, particularly in instances of workplace bullying, damages may be awarded in lieu of the notice period to which the employee would otherwise have been entitled under his contract. This is very important if an employee's contract provides a more generous notice period than that for which he or she would otherwise be entitled to compensation under statute. Alternatively, where there is no such notice period expressed at all in the contract or where there is a dispute about same, a civil court will imply a reasonable notice period into the contract. This period may, depending on the seniority or status of an employee and his period of service within a particular business, equally amount to more than that which the employee may otherwise have been entitled to under statute. Finally, like any claim for breach of contract, the employee has six years within which to commence wrongful dismissal proceedings.

'Unfair'

On the other hand, a Rights Commissioner or the EAT **cannot** apply the terms of a private contract. They can only apply the entitlements and reliefs provided for in legislation. Therefore, in this case, an employee is simply seeking his entitlements under statute. As such, an order of compensation, re-engagement or reinstatement may be made. The advantages are that it is informal and relatively less expensive than the ordinary courts. In particular, each party to a dispute pays only his own costs.

However, the claim must be brought within six months of the resignation unless there are exceptional circumstances that prevented it being made within this period, in which case, the period is extended to twelve months. [17]

Moreover, there is a cap on the maximum amount of compensation that may be awarded to a claimant for an unfair dismissal. It cannot exceed 104 weeks gross remuneration for the job from which he or she was dismissed. It is also based on the financial loss attributable to the dismissal as is just and equitable in all the circumstances. Since 1993, even where an employee can show no financial loss attributable

[17] *Grady v. Royal Bank Of Scotland,* EAT, July, 2002.

to the dismissal, the EAT still now has a discretion to award compensation equal to four weeks remuneration at the most.

An employee must also have **one year's continuous service** before he can take a claim. The employee must, finally, show that he was constructively dismissed within the meaning of the Act. There are two ways to do this.

Firstly, he or she may argue that the conduct of the employer entitled him or her to resign. This may occur where an employer so conducts himself as to show that he does not intend to be bound by the contract of employment. A Rights Commissioner or the EAT will have regard to the nature of the employment relationship between the parties and to those requirements essential to all employment agreements, in particular, the need for mutual trust and confidence in the workplace. However, unlike in wrongful dismissal claims, they can only provide a statutory remedy rather than enforce any entitlements under the contract itself.

Secondly, even if an employee cannot show his or her entitlement to resign, he or she will ask the Tribunal or a Rights Commissioner to look at the surrounding circumstances and conclude that it was reasonable for him or her to do so.

Either one of these arguments, if decided in favour of the employee, will result in a finding of constructive dismissal.

However, in certain cases, a Rights Commissioner or the EAT may rule against an employee on the basis that the action he took by resigning, without recourse to a grievance procedure, was precipitous.

The caselaw

A selection of some of the important and most recent cases in this area demonstrates the type of conduct employers should avoid in their workplaces.

Byrne v. RHM Foods (Ireland) Ltd. *Workplace Isolation: A freeze-out or a cooling off?*[18]

This was a seminal case before the EAT. The claimant was employed as the personal secretary to the Respondent's Marketing Manager. The Marketing Manager was suspended from employment in circumstances that resulted in an emotive atmosphere for all concerned and, particularly, for the Manager Director who assumed the duties of the Marketing Manager at that time. In the aftermath of the suspension, there was a severe and sudden cooling-off of her working relationships. The claimant was given absolutely no work to do and she received no further contact from the Managing Director or anyone on his behalf. She was left in isolation. She felt she was being studiously avoided. The claimant's telephone was disconnected during this period. Within six to seven weeks of the suspension, she was certified as suffering 'nervous strain'. The EAT found in favour of the claimant. While not holding that there was a 'freeze out' policy adopted by the respondent, they were unanimously of the view that the total isolation of the claimant amounted to an undermining of the relationship of trust and confidence between the parties, such as went to the root of the contract. This entitled her to claim that she was constructively dismissed and it was so determined.

Wyse v. St Margaret's Country Club Ltd. *Ill-defined jobs: From run-ins to walk-outs!*[19]

This recent case deals with the consequences for employers of allowing hostilities and aggression to develop between employees brought about by ill-defined or unclear task and role specifications. The facts of this case are particularly

[18] UD 69/1979.
[19] UD 577/1999.

important. The respondent employed the claimant as a kitchen porter. One particular morning, whilst walking through the kitchen of the respondent's premises and engaged on another task, she alleged that she was aggressively questioned by the Chef as to why she had failed to arrive and remain in the kitchen in order to prepare sandwiches for a social event being organised by the respondent for that evening. However, no one had told her that she had been required there and, when she spoke to her supervisor, the complainant was only then told that she was indeed needed in the kitchen. However, she felt that the Chef had verbally abused her unfairly. She had also encountered problems with his hostile attitude in the two weeks leading up to the incident. She further claimed that she felt he was a bully. As a result, she told her employer that morning that she was leaving, there and then, and walked out of her job.

At the hearing of the claim, the respondent accepted that there had been confusion over the roster. It was a very busy morning and the Chef had been under tremendous pressure. Furthermore, he was primarily responsible for the catering at that time as the Head-Chef had also previously left and had not yet been replaced. There were ninety people arriving that evening and he had been left without the assistance of the claimant in making preparations for them. A representative of the respondent before the Tribunal submitted that she had spoken to the Chef later that day in order to 'patch things up.'

The Tribunal agreed that the claimant's decision to walk out of her job arose because of her being verbally abused by the chef for not working in the kitchen on that particular morning. It was accepted that she was naturally upset at the way she had been treated and that when she complained she was merely told to have a cup of tea. It also accepted that the confusion and misunderstanding over the roster was the respondent's fault. However, the issue came down to whether the complainant was entitled to resign from her job there and then. On consideration of the evidence, it decided that she was unfairly dismissed. However, the Tribunal considered that her actions had contributed to her dismissal and awarded her £1,000 in compensation having made an appropriate (but unspecified) deduction.

Allen v. Independent Newspapers (Irl) Ltd. *Workplace bullying hits the front page!*[20]

The background

This 2001 decision is one of the most important cases yet in Ireland on stress and bullying in the workplace. The claimant, Ms Allen, a high-profile journalist, was employed as the crime correspondent of the respondent from August 1996 to September 2000. She alleged before the EAT that she had been subjected to continuous harassment and bullying and that she had been effectively isolated at work. This conduct undermined her confidence and health to such a degree that she could no longer tolerate her working environment and was left with no option but to resign. It was also alleged that the conduct of the respondent had led, not only to her constructive dismissal, but also to illness. In particular, the claimant had suffered serious work-related stress symptoms including sleeplessness, palpitations, nervousness, headaches, poor-appetite, concentration loss and associated difficulties and loss of confidence. As a result, she also claimed that she had been and remained unfit for work following her resignation. Accordingly, Ms Allen had also instituted parallel High Court personal injury proceedings.

---

20 UD 641/2000.

The bullying

The many instances of alleged bullying in this case may be summarised briefly by the following:

> **Co-employees:** The conduct and treatment of her by some fellow employees was alleged to be hostile, intimidating and humiliating. In particular, this included ignoring her, refusing to communicate with her and, on one occasion, a cigarette was hurled towards her.
>
> **Job insecurity and role conflict:** Several events are important under this heading. In August 1999, the complainant was requested to write a social diary column unconnected with matters ever covered by a crime correspondent. She was unwilling to do this. This further damaged her relationship with the Editor. She was also directed to attend at the offices of the newspaper at times that were alleged to be inconsistent, in conflict or inconvenient with her job as a crime correspondent. In August 2000, a new journalist was recruited and assigned crime related stories that the claimant felt was to her detriment. In September 2000, there was a formal event to welcome this new journalist, at which point, the complainant alleged that she felt like 'an invisible person'.
>
> **The superiors and employer:** In September 1999, the claimant had a meeting with her immediate supervisor to specifically inform him of the hostility and negativity in the workplace. She informed him that his failure to deal with it would result in her having a nervous breakdown. However, her situation remained unacknowledged and her morale began to suffer. Her loss of confidence was such that she even began to find it difficult to use the telephone in the course of

her employment. In January 2000, she advised her employer that she intended to take sixteen days leave in the upcoming Spring in order to work on a book. However, she was sent a letter in April 2000 taking issue with the 'unprecedented accumulation' of days off and warning her that failure to attend at the office during the specified periods would constitute absence from work and would be recorded as such on her attendance record. The claimant alleged that this was entirely at variance with what had been agreed at the commencement of her employment. The claimant had three further meetings with her supervisors regarding the hostility. The first in May 2000, a second with the group managing editor in June 2000 and another with the group managing editor in September 2000. After this latter meeting, she resigned and claimed constructive dismissal before the EAT.

The decision

She was awarded £70,500 in compensation (equating to 78 weeks gross remuneration) and, in an extremely important decision, this included future financial loss due to the work-related stress injuries.

The lessons?

This decision has two significant implications for employers.

Grievance procedures

Firstly, there are circumstances when an employee does not now have to invoke an available grievance procedure before claiming constructive dismissal. In particular, if an employer perpetrates or knows of bullying against a particular employee and leaves it unchecked or unacknowledged, then the fact that an employee does not invoke a grievance procedure available to him may not be fatal to a constructive dismissal claim. In Allen, there was evidence submitted that workplace complaints could have been dealt with by either going to the National Union of Journalists ('NUJ') or directly to management. The respondent had argued that it was incumbent on the complainant, before resigning, to invoke the NUJ procedure. However, the EAT concluded:

> "The objective of utilising the NUJ grievance procedure would have been to bring the claimant's grievances to the attention of the respondent. The Tribunal is, however, satisfied that, at various stages throughout her employment ... Ms Allen brought her complaints to senior management level within the respondent newspaper."

Compensation awards

Secondly, employers are now potentially exposed in bullying and harassment cases to higher compensation awards by the EAT. Under the 1977 Act (as amended), the financial loss suffered by an employee, whether actual or future must be attributable to the dismissal before it can be compensated. Allen is authority for the argument that, in constructive dismissal claims, there are circumstances when a future loss of earnings, caused by work-related stress suffered before the dismissal, is also attributable to the actual dismissal and may now be compensated accordingly.

In other words, an employee with a psychiatric injury, alleged to have been suffered through work-related bullying and stress, can claim that, because it is attributable wholly to the same conduct that also led to the constructive dismissal, then his loss of future earnings is now equally attributable to the employer in the event that he remains unfit to return to work.[21]

Indeed, the Unfair Dismissals Act 1977 (as amended) itself seems to reinforce such an approach when it provides that regard shall be had to the extent to which the financial loss was attributable to an act, omission or conduct by or on behalf of the employer. [22]

However, from the perspective of employers, this entire approach may be criticised for two reasons.

In the first instance, such losses are arguably not attributable to the dismissal at all as required under statute but to a pre-dismissal injury or illness only. Moreover, an employee has a remedy for these psychiatric illnesses already by way of damages for a personal injury at common law (see Chapter 2).

In the second instance, Allen allows for the imposing on employers of a liability to compensate workers for stress and bullying related injury in circumstances when it would not be imposed in the civil courts at common law. The test in Allen is that the illness must be **wholly attributable to the same conduct** that gave rise to the resignation. On this basis, once a tribunal were to satisfy itself that the conduct and associated working conditions justified the resignation of the employee, then the issue would simply come down to a matter of proving as fact the necessary connection between the illness and the conduct. There is little scope for the vital requirement of the civil courts that the employer must also reasonably foresee the injury before liability attaches.

---

[21] Authority for the *Allen* decision was the Irish Supreme Court judgment of *Carney v. Balkan Tours Ltd.* [1997] 1 I.R. 153; the English case of *Devine v. Designer Flowers Wholesale Florist Sundries Ltd* [1993] I.R.L.R. 517; the English case of *Hilton International Hotels (UK) Ltd v. Faraji* [1994] I.R.L.R. 265.

[22] Section 7(2) of Unfair Dismissals Act 1977(as amended).

Post-Allen?

Therefore, the clear distinction in bullying cases between work-related stress and unfair dismissal has become blurred and may be breaking down. If so, it is an interesting, although from an employer's perspective, discomforting development. On the other hand, the facts and the nature of the Allen case may ultimately prove it to be a legal anomaly rather than a general rule. However, a further determination of the EAT in Ireland in 2002 has again expanded the traditional basis for awarding compensation in bullying and harassment claims resulting in an increasing financial exposure to liability for employers.[23] This further indicates that it is unlikely that Allen is going to be simply an isolated award.

Moreover, an English decision of the House of Lords has now unequivocally confirmed a fundamental shift in the approach to compensating work-related stress in successful unfair dismissal claims along similar lines to Allen.

Johnson v. Unisys Limited. *A judgment reverberating through tribunal corridors across the land*[24]

Background

Mr Johnson started working for Unisys Limited, an international software company, in 1971. At the end of 1985, he suffered a psychological illness brought on by work-related stress. He was prescribed anti-depressants by his doctor and had to take time off work. In 1994, he was summarily dismissed for some alleged irregularity. He complained to an employment tribunal for unfair dismissal and it upheld his claim. It was found that the company had not given him a

---

[23] See Chapter 5: *Browne v. Ventelo Ltd,* UD 597/2001.
[24] [2001] U.K.H.L. 13.

fair opportunity to defend himself and had not complied with its own disciplinary procedures. Some two years later, Mr Johnson commenced a claim for damages against the company at common law on the grounds of breach of contract and negligence. He argued that as a consequence of both the fact of dismissal and the manner it was done, he had suffered a nervous breakdown that affected his family life and had made it impossible for him to find work. He became depressed, attempted suicide and started to drink heavily. In 1994, he had spent five months in a mental hospital and had been readmitted there on occasion since then. He considered that he would never find remunerated employment again and estimated his loss of earnings to be in excess of STG£400,000. He instituted proceedings that ultimately ended up before the House of Lords.

Judgment

The Plaintiff's appeal to the Law Lords was rejected. However, this is not the important point. This is because the rejection was expressly not on the basis of the grounds on which he was seeking compensation. Indeed, on that point, his right was upheld. In particular, it was held that:

> "[h]is most substantial claim is of financial loss flowing from his psychiatric injury which he says was a consequence of the unfair manner of his dismissal. Such a loss is a consequence of the dismissal which may form the subject matter of a compensatory award...The emphasis is upon the Tribunal awarding such compensation as it thinks just and equitable."

Therefore, although not directly dealing with a constructive dismissal, this judgment has supported the approach adopted in cases like Allen in that it accepts that psychiatric illness and injury is rightfully a factor within the scope of what is just and equitable for unfair dismissal compensation. As a result, it equally has important implications for the manner in which all such cases (especially constructive dismissal claims for bullying) may be compensated over the coming years.

Conclusions

It was a feature of *Johnson*, and a possible future direction for Irish employment law, that the English legislation being interpreted by the court, unlike the statutes still in place in Ireland, has removed the condition of 'financial loss' and replaced it simply with the condition of 'loss'. This 'loss' must be attributable to action taken by the employer.[25] Therefore, in the course of the decision, and, in what was described as a 'comment that will reverberate through tribunal corridors across the land', it was confirmed that this 'loss' now also permits compensation to be awarded in England for the distress, humiliation, damage to reputation in the community or to family life as a result of dismissal. However, from an Irish perspective, it is important that the psychiatric illness claim was dealt with solely in the context of financial loss.

Therefore, like so many other areas of work-related stress liability highlighted throughout this book, compensation for unfair dismissal (with particular reference to the constructive dismissal claim based on bullying) is another area in which significant development is certain to occur over the coming years. The absorption of stress-related illness into the unfair dismissal scenario is particularly crucial. As such, employers and their advisers must now both incorporate these present developments and prepare for and keep abreast of the

[25] Section 123(1) of the Employment Rights Act 1996 (UK).

doubtless unrelenting and creeping advance of the employer liability compensation regime.

3. The health and safety route

This route involves an employee relying on the Safety, Health and Welfare at Work Act 1989 and the regulations made under it. The Act provides that it is the duty of every employer, insofar as reasonably practicable, to protect the safety, health and welfare of employees at work. The common law rules on this area (negligence, breach of contract) were dealt with in Chapter 2. Moreover, even prior to the introduction of the Code of Practice on Bullying, the 1989 Act and the regulations made under it were considered to include matters relating to workplace bullying and harassment.[26]

Civil proceedings unlikely for a breach of the act alone

Although quite revolutionary in its day, the biggest weakness of the 1989 Act remains the fact that there is no specific civil redress or sanctions provided by it that may be imposed whenever it is breached. In particular, none of the specific obligations under the Act give an employee a statutory entitlement to civil compensation and many only provide a cause of action in criminal proceedings. Furthermore, none relate specifically to stress and bullying in the workplace. Nevertheless, there are some useful provisions that give rise to a civil cause of action. Instances where a breach may be pleaded in a civil claim include, in particular, where an employer does not prepare a safety statement or where he or she is not in possession of a risk assessment in writing of the

---

[26] Section 6(1) of the Safety, Health and Welfare at Work Act 1989. Also para. (g) of the First Schedule to the Act states its intent to develop a policy of prevention covering (among others) social relationships and the influence of factors related to the working environment.

hazards to health and safety in the workplace. Regulations implemented to extend the Act also give rise to civil causes of action, in particular, the failure by an employer to provide health and safety information and training to employees. Finally, we have already seen earlier that, if the Irish courts were to follow *Cross v. Highland and Island Enterprises* in the future then it is strongly arguable that, for the first time, there is an express duty of care on employers to have an assessment in writing of the specific hazards associated with work-related stress: see Chapter 2.

However, the civil claim in which employers most normally face allegations of a breach of the 1989 Act is in relation to personal injury claims for damages. This is because the civil courts will take all such statutory breaches into account when deciding on any award of damages to make. As a result, in order to be financially compensated for any breaches of the health and safety legislation, an employee must inevitably bring the entire process back to the pursuit of a personal injury claim.

In short, health and safety legislation piggybacks on the common law system and any breaches of it are invariably pleaded as part of a general personal injury claim rather than as an independent breach of statute claim.

A new opportunity for the whistle-blower

Another weakness of this area is the fact that the health and safety legislation provides no specific forum to an employee bullied in the workplace. In particular, the Health and Safety Authority cannot investigate complaints or get involved in individual allegations. However, if, in the workplace, there is no system at all for the prevention and investigation of bullying in line with the Code of Practice, the employee may then complain to the Authority and it can request an employer to put such mechanisms in place as to ensure that an employee has a fair procedure available to him. This may be in the form of an anti-bullying policy related to the Safety Statement.

In keeping with this approach, the Authority has issued a booklet for employees on guidelines for preventing workplace bullying and it has now established a Bullying Response Unit with direct access to the public.[27]

Criminal sanctions

Finally, in very serious cases of bullying, such as violence or physical attacks directed at an employee, an employer should never discount the prospect that the Authority might indeed bring criminal proceedings against him or her under the appropriate procedures of the 1989 Act.

Since March 2002, the Authority has signalled to employers that the criminal law is an increasingly important part of its anti-bullying armoury. Employers must specifically remember that the Code of Practice on Workplace Bullying and its incorporated anti-bullying policy and procedures are now admissible in evidence in criminal proceedings where they give practical guidance to a court in deciding the guilt of an employer.

However, getting a criminal conviction for a work-related stress injury, as distinct from work-related acts of physical violence, is particularly difficult.

Finally, where an employee dismisses an employee wholly or mainly as a result of any of the relevant civil or criminal proceedings discussed in this chapter being taken against him or her, whether actual, threatened or proposed, in which the employee is either a party or likely to be a witness, then that may be deemed an 'unfair dismissal' and will constitute a separate and fresh claim before the EAT.[28]

---

[27] *Guidelines on the Prevention of Workplace Bullying*, Health and Safety Authority, Dublin, 2002.

[28] Section 6(2)(c) and (4) of the Unfair Dismissals Act 1977(as amended).

In more recent times, there have also been many new legislative developments and innovations since the introduction of the 1989 Act. This is particularly so in the areas of harassment and sexual harassment.

Therefore, these innovations and their implications for the workplace are matters that will now be examined over the course of the next chapter.

CHAPTER 4

Harassment: An Insidious Form of Workplace Discrimination

GENERAL OVERVIEW

The legal basis

This area is governed by the Employment Equality Act 1998.[1] This Act prohibits discrimination in relation to an individual's employment whereby he or she is treated less favourably on one or more of nine specified grounds. It applies not only to an employer but also to employment agencies, trade unions, employer bodies and professional and trade organisations.

Under the Act, harassment is a *specific form* of discrimination in relation to the conditions of employment based on one or more of those nine grounds. In particular, sexual harassment is a form of gender discrimination. Furthermore, since March 2002, there is now a *Code of Practice on Sexual Harassment and Harassment at Work* in existence. This Code has legal effect. This means that not only is it admissible in evidence before a court or equality officer but if any provision of the code appears to be relevant to any question arising in the proceedings, it shall be taken into account in determining that question.[2]

---

1 Employment Equality Act 1998 (Code of Practice)(Harassment) Order 2002 (S.I. No. 78 of 2002); also, *Code of Practice on Sexual Harassment and Harassment at Work,* The Equality Authority, Dublin, March 2002. This chapter reflects and contains advice and recommendations of this Code of Practice.

2 Employment Equality Act 1998, s. 56.

The relationship between harassment and bullying

Like bullying, harassment has no specific meaning in common law. Therefore, in civil proceedings for wrongful dismissal or personal injury, a claim for 'harassment and bullying' generally will normally be pleaded in order to ensure that the entirety of the inappropriate behaviour alleged by an employee is caught by a claim. As will be seen, harassment may also be identified and minimised in the workplace in much the same way as bullying.

However, what is new and different is that, since the 1998 Act, a defined concept of 'harassment' has been created with distinct entitlements and a specific regime for employees to challenge harassing behaviour, as a wrong in itself, when it is based on one of nine grounds under the Act even if the employee is not injured or dismissed. In simple terms, harassment may now be considered as simply a specific form of bullying linked to on one or more nine grounds specified by the 1998 Act.

However, unlike bullying, a *single* incident may constitute harassment or sexual harassment. Bullying not based on one of the nine grounds was dealt with in chapter three.

'SEXUAL HARASSMENT'

The definition

Sexual harassment is a specific form of discrimination on the grounds of gender but with a sexual motivation. As such, it is given separate treatment from gender discrimination generally under the Act. Harassment on the gender ground without a sexual motivation may be dealt with as harassment generally (see next section).

Sexual harassment occurs where:

- There is any act of physical intimacy by B towards A, or any request by B for sexual favours from A, or any other act or conduct of B (including, without limitation, spoken words, gestures, or the production, display or circulation of written words, pictures or other material);

  and

  The act, request or conduct is unwelcome by A **and** could reasonably be regarded as sexually, or otherwise on the gender ground, offensive, humiliating or intimidating to A.[3]

- 'A' and 'B' represent two persons of the opposite sex so that where 'A' is a woman, 'B' is a man and *vice versa*.[4]

Same-sex harassment is not covered by this definition. In other words, the harasser must be of the opposite sex to the victim.

The location

An employee may be sexually harassed either:

> **In the workplace**; or
>
> Is subjected **outside the workplace** to work-related harassment.[5]

Examples

Physical conduct of a sexual nature

This conduct may include ***unwelcome*** physical contact such as unnecessary:

---

[3] Section 23(3).
[4] Section 18(1).
[5] Section 23(1).

- Touching;
- Patting;
- Pinching;
- Brushing against another employee's body;
- Assault; or
- Coercive sexual intercourse.

Verbal conduct of a sexual nature

This includes behaviour such as ***unwelcome***:

- Sexual advances;
- Propositions;
- Pressure for sexual activity;
- Continued suggestions for social activity outside of the workplace after it has been made clear that such suggestions are unwelcome;
- Unwanted or offensive flirtations and suggestive remarks;
- Lewd innuendo and comments.

Non-verbal conduct of a sexual nature

This may include the display of pornographic or sexually suggestive:

- Pictures;
- Objects;
- Written materials;
- E-mails;
- Faxes; or
- Mobile telephone text-messages.

Sex-Based Conduct

This includes conduct that denigrates, ridicules or is intimidatory or physically abusive of an employee because of his or her gender. This may comprise of derogatory or degrading abuse or insults that are gender-related.[6]

'Harassment'

Harassment is any act or conduct including spoken words, gestures or the production, display or circulation of written words, pictures or other material, if the conduct is unwelcome to the employee and could reasonably be regarded as offensive, humiliating or intimidating.[7]

This definition is the same as that for sexual harassment but without the sexual element. The harassment has to be based on or motivated by one or more of the nine relevant characteristic of the employee targeted. These are: [8]

- Marital Status;
- Age;
- Sexual Orientation.
- Family Status;
- Race;
- Gender;
- Religious belief;
- Disability;

---

6 The above examples are provided in the *Code of Practice on Sexual Harassment and Harassment At Work* Equality Authority, Dublin 2002.

7 Section 32(5).

8 Section 6(2).

- Membership of the Travelling Community.

The location

If an employee may be harassed either:

> **In the workplace**; or
>
> Is subjected **outside the workplace** to work-related harassment.[9]

Assumptions

The protection of the Act extends to situations where the employee does not have the relevant characteristic but the **harasser believes** that he or she has that characteristic. [10]

Two examples

Where the harasser is a religious bigot who believes that the targeted employee either is of a different faith or denomination or holds *no* religious belief when that is not correct. When the harasser believes that the employee targeted is gay when he or she is not.

Attributes

Example

An employee is protected when he is harassed not about his race directly (such as his national or ethnic origin) but about some other physical or social feature referable to belonging to that race such as skin or hair colour, height or accent.

---

[9] Section 32(2).
[10] Section 32(1).

Similarly, a religious belief may not be targeted directly by the harasser but instead he or she may base the harassment on a dietary regime or dress code associated with and required by it. In this case, an employee is also protected.

Therefore, a wide range of behaviour, when related to one or more of the nine grounds, may constitute harassment. It may include: [11]

- Verbal harassment: Jokes, comments, ridicule or songs.
- Physical harassment: Jostling, shoving or any form of assault.
- Written harassment: Faxes, e-mails, text messages, bulletins or notices.
- Intimidatory harassment: Gestures, posturing or intimidatory poses.
- Isolation or exclusion from social activities.
- Pressure to behave in a manner that the employee thinks is inappropriate. For example, a requirement to dress in a manner unsuited to a person's ethnic or religious background or belief.

Proving the Claim

Apart from the difference outlined above, both a claim for sexual harassment and harassment (without a sexual element) share the same common elements for the purposes of proof and attributing liability.

---

[11] *Code of Practice on Sexual Harassment and Harassment At Work* Equality Authority, Dublin 2002 at pp.8 and 9.

The two ingredients

The test for proving harassment or sexual harassment contains a subjective and an objective element. This means that an employee must show that the conduct is unwelcome **and** is to be reasonably regarded as offensive, humiliating or threatening.[12]

Unwelcome

Each employee must decide:

(a) What behaviour is unwelcome to them, irrespective of the attitude of others to the matter;

(b) From whom, if anyone, such behaviour is welcome or unwelcome, irrespective of the attitude of others to the matter.

The fact that an individual has previously agreed with or acquiesced in the behaviour does not prevent him or her from deciding that it has now become unwelcome.

'Reasonably be regarded'

This is the same test as for bullying dealt with earlier in this Guide. This means that even if the conduct complained of is unwelcome, it must not be so trivial or insignificant that a reasonable, objective employee would not consider it offensive, humiliating or intimidating. Although an employee must decide what is unwelcome, irrespective of the attitude of others, he or she must, nonetheless, cross this threshold before his claim is capable of succeeding.

This helps to protect employers from vexatious claims. It also protects them from claims by employees who may be

[12] Section 23(3)(sex harassment); s. 32(5) (harassment).

unreasonably sensitive, conservative or modest. However, as with bullying generally, the employer must be careful not to overlook conduct simply because he himself does not believe it to constitute harassment, if an employee brings it to the attention of the business or complains about it.

Is the intention of the harasser important?

The intention of the perpetrator of the sexual harassment or harassment is not relevant to succeeding in a claim. The fact that an alleged perpetrator did not have the intention of sexually harassing or harassing the employee is not a defence. It is the *effect* of the behaviour on the employee that is important.

Respecting and understanding boundaries and differences

Therefore, sexual, personal or social relationships between male and female employees, in the workplace are, of course, not prohibited by the rules about gender.

Equally, the diversity and differences among employees in the workplace across the other eight grounds will and should continue to be positively expressed. It is the unwanted, negative, offensive nature of conduct that distinguishes sexual harassment and harassment from friendly behaviour that is welcome and mutual.

Differences are not a threat to the workplace, only the manner in which they are handled. The purpose of the 1998 Act is simply to protect and to promote respect for and understanding of diversity in the workplace.

One example

In the increasingly multi-cultural Ireland, it will not be unusual, in the coming years, for employees in a single workplace to support a variety of international football teams by virtue of their national or ethnic origin. Whereas, in a context of intolerance and prejudice, difference becomes a source of confrontation and contention, such games and tournaments are a good example of how good-natured and welcome, albeit competitive, banter and behaviour arising out of diverse and differing loyalties become a positive experience. Similarly, under Irish law and health and safety practice, diversity as a positive experience will be the mark of a successful working environment. Indeed, paradoxically, diversity may ultimately serve to enhance the solidarity of a workplace.

Employers failing to grasp this fundamental social reality will now suffer both legally by provoking an increased risk of litigation and financially through poor staff morale and high staff turnover.

Who are the Harassers?

The 1998 Act protects employees from harassment by: [13]

- An employer;
- Fellow employees;
- Clients of the business;
- Customers; or
- Other business contacts. This includes any person with whom the employer might reasonably expect the employee to come into contact with in the workplace.

These may include those who supply or deliver goods or services to the employer, maintenance and other types of professional or trade contractors as well as any volunteers, interns and persons on work-experience.

---

[13] Sections 23(1), 32(1), 23(4), 32(2).

The Scope of the Prohibition

Location

The scope of sexual harassment and harassment reaches beyond the workplace to work-related events or events that are attended by employees in the course of their employment. Therefore, conferences and training seminars that occur outside the workplace are covered. It may also extend to work-related social events. This may be particularly so if they are arranged and organised officially by an employer.

Different treatment

The protection extends to where an employee is treated differently in the course of his or her employment because he or she has either rejected or accepted the sexual harassment or harassment. Examples of such different treatment may be related to decisions taken concerning the employee's promotion, access to training or salary. Where an employee is treated differently in this way, it constitutes another, fresh act of harassment or sexual harassment.[14]

Other situations covered

The law prohibiting harassment and sexual harassment also applies to students or persons in vocational training. It also applies to employment agencies.[15]

---

[14] Sections 23(2)(b) and 32(2)(b).
[15] Sections 23(6). and 32(7.)

WHAT DEFENCES ARE AVAILABLE TO EMPLOYERS?

Obligations of the Employer

The 1998 Act requires employers to act in a preventative and remedial way. Under the Act, employers are legally responsible for the harassment and sexual harassment carried out by any of the persons outlined above. [16]

Reasonably practicable steps

It is a defence for an employer to prove that he or she took reasonably practicable steps to prevent:

- The particular employee (or the general category of employees sharing his relevant characteristic) being sexually harassed or harassed; and
- The particular employee (or the general category of employees sharing his relevant characteristic) being treated differently in the workplace or in the course of employment, and insofar as any such treatment has already occurred, to reverse its effects.[17]

In practice, in order to rely on this defence, an employer, first of all, will have to show that he or she has comprehensive, accessible, effective policies that focus on prevention, best practice, remedial action and an accessible, effective complaints procedure. Secondly, the steps taken to put the policies and procedures into real effect will also be taken into account.

An employer will not be able to rely on an excellent policy if it has not been effectively and **meaningfully implemented.**

---

[16] Section 15(1).

[17] Sections 15(3), 23(5) and 32(6).

Where a Claim against you may be Heard

As we saw earlier, sexual harassment or harassment, like bullying generally, is a recognised and identifiable source of work-related stress. Therefore, if the nature or duration of the harassment is such that the levels of stress suffered damage the psychiatric health of an employee or result in personal injuries in any way (perhaps through physical violence), the employee may always bring proceedings for *damages* in the civil courts. This was dealt with in Chapter 2. However, even if there are no such personal injuries alleged, the employee may now seek redress exclusively for breach of his or her statutory rights under the 1998 Act. The remedies available include, in particular, compensation, reinstatement or re-engagement.

Depending on the nature of the act(s) of sexual harassment or harassment and whether the employee wishes to deal with the breach formally or informally, the employer may end up in any one of the following: [18]

The Office of the Director of Equality Investigations:

A complaint of sexual harassment or harassment on any other grounds may be made to this Office. The Office may refer the claim to an **Equality Officer**, or, with the agreement of both parties, for **mediation** by an equality mediation officer. The 1998 Act provides for a specific statutory mediation service.[19]

The Labour Court

The Labour Court *exclusively* hears all dismissal claims (including constructive dismissal) arising out of any of the

[18] Sections 74 to 93.

[19] Sections 75(7) and 78(1), (2) and (3).

prohibitions under the 1998 Act. Where it appears to this Court that a matter may be resolved by mediation it may also adopt this approach, if both parties are agreeable, either within its own structure or by referring it back to an equality mediation officer. [20]

The Circuit Court

In sexual harassment claims (and **all** claims on the gender ground), the employee may bypass the above two bodies and refer the matter directly to the appropriate Circuit Court. [21] The court Circuit in which the claim is brought must be the one covering the geographic area where the employer resides or carries on any business, profession or occupation.[22]

The Time Limits and Remedies

Time limits

A complaint must be made within six months of the alleged incident of sexual harassment or harassment *or of the latest incident* of such behaviour to which the claim relates. This may be extended to up to twelve months where exceptional circumstances prevented the making of the complaint within the original six months. This six-month period applies in taking a claim to the Director, to the Labour Court and to the Circuit Court.[23] In the latter case, the normal limitation period of six years for breach of employment contract cases does **not** apply.

---

[20] Sections 77(2) and 78(2). The EAT has **NO JURISDICTION** to hear unfair dismissal claims made under the 1998 Act.

[21] Section 77(3).

[22] Section 80(2).

[23] Section 77(6).

Compensation

The maximum amount that can be awarded by either the Office of the Director of Equality Investigations or by the Labour Court is 104 weeks remuneration *as received* or, where it is greater, 104 weeks remuneration that the employee *would have received* had there not been any discrimination or victimisation in the workplace.[24] The 1998 Act also expressly provides that enactments relating to the jurisdiction of the Circuit Court are not to be taken as limiting the amount of compensation that may be awarded by that Court in claims under the 1998 Act.[25] This means that the normal jurisdictional limit of the Circuit Court, namely €38,000 (£30,000), is not applicable. In terms of compensation, this is the most serious situation an employer may, therefore, find himself in.

Reinstatement or re-engagement

In the event of a dismissal, the Labour Court or the Circuit Court may order a reinstatement or a re-engagement, with or without compensation, as appropriate.[26] The Circuit Court will primarily come into contact with a dismissal claim under the 1998 Act either *at first instance* when the dismissal is alleged to be on the grounds of gender or *on appeal* from a decision of the Labour Court.

Equal treatment or other specified course of action

Section 82 of the 1998 Act also provides that redress may take the form of a specified course of action to remedy the

---

[24] Section 82(4).
[25] Section 82(3).
[26] Section 82(2) and (3).

harassment complained of. What these may be will depend on the circumstance of each individual case.[27]

Criminal conviction

An employer may also be criminally convicted under the 1998 Act. He or she may be prosecuted summarily by a District Justice or on indictment before a jury. On conviction, he may be fined or imprisoned or both. [28]

Two offences draw the serious implications of a criminal prosecution. Firstly, if an employer dismisses an employee for seeking relief or otherwise relying on his entitlements under the Act. This is known as '*victimisation*' and is dealt with below. Victimisation may also be dealt with under civil sanctions. Secondly, an employer who obstructs or impedes the Labour Court, the Office of the Director or one of its Equality Officers or otherwise fails to comply with one of their requirements in the course of the proceedings, is also guilty of a criminal offence and is at risk of prosecution.[29]

Right of appeal

From Director to Labour Court

The decision of an Equality Officer (under the rubric of the Director of Equality Investigations) may be appealed by either the respondent or the applicant not later than 42 days **from** *the date* **of the decision** by notice in writing to the Labour Court specifying the grounds of appeal. In the course of hearing that appeal, the Labour Court may refer a point of law to the High Court and adjourn the appeal pending an

---

[27] Section 82(1)(d) and (e).
[28] Section 100.
[29] Section 98(1) and (8).

answer.[30] Moreover, where the Labour Court makes a determination on an appeal from a decision of the Director of Equality Investigations, the **only** further appeal, therefter, appears in practice to be on a point of law to the High Court. In other words, **no appeal** will lie in this circumstance to the Circuit Court. A further appeal would then only lie to the Supreme Court from the decision of the High Court on that point of law. It is suggested that, as no rules of court have yet been made on this issue, any such appeals or references to the High Court on a point of law be made by way of special summons by analogy with the procedures set out in Orders 105 and 106 of the Rules of the Superior Courts 1986. As such, this type of appeal must be lodged within 21 days of this determination of the Labour Court (although there is provision in the above Orders for this to be extended to 42 days in exceptional circumstances).[31]

From Labour Court to Circuit Court

Where dispute under the 1998 Act is referred **in the first instance** to the Labour Court the decision of the Labour Court may be appealed to the Circuit Court by either party not later than 42 days **from** *the date* **of the determination** of the Labour Court or such further time as the Circuit Court may allow. The decision of the Circuit Court is final and conclusive. However, this is subject to an appeal by either party to the High Court on a point of law only.[32]

How decisions and settlements are enforced by the law

Where the employer fails to comply with a **final deter-**

---

30 Sections 83(1) and 90(4).

31 Kerr, Anthony, *Employment Equality Legislation* (section 30 annotation generally, 2001 Edition, Dublin, Round Hall Ltd, 2001).

32 Section 90(1) and (2).

mination of the Director or the Labour Court an application can be brought by the employee to the Circuit Court and it shall make an order directing the carrying out of the decision of either the Director or the Labour Court in accordance with its terms. This application cannot be made before the time allowed to appeal the decision has expired (see below).[33]

Where the parties agree to **a mediated settlement** of a claim and one of the parties has failed to give effect to the terms of the settlement, in whole or in part, then an application can be brought to the Circuit Court and it shall make an order directing the carrying out of the settlement in its entirety. However, the Circuit Court cannot enforce any aspect of this mediated settlement agreed between the parties that could not have been provided as a relief under the 1998 Act. This application cannot be made before the expiry of 42 days from the date of the written record of the settlement.[34]

The Circuit Court, when asked to enforce a decision or mediated settlement in this way, can actually make **additional orders** to punish an employer for failing to comply.[35]

This Court can also, where it considers appropriate, make an order **substituting the earlier decision** of an Equality Officer or of the Labour Court to re-engage or reinstate an employee for an order of compensation instead. The maximum compensation that may be awarded in this way *in lieu of reinstatement or re-engagement* is calculated on the same basis as provided above.[36]

The failure of an employer to comply with an order of the Circuit Court is contempt of court and may result in **imprisonment**.

---

[33] Section 91(1) and (3).
[34] Section 91(2) and (4).
[35] Section 92.
[36] Section 93.

RIGHTS AFFORDED AN EMPLOYEE WHO COMPLAINS

Material information

Prior to making a complaint under the 1998 Act, an employee is entitled to seek from the employer "material information" in his or her possession about:

- The alleged acts of sexual harassment or harassment at issue;
- The failure of the employer to deal with them;
- The relevant workplace procedures.

Information relating to a particular individual and which so identifies him or her cannot be disclosed without the consent of that individual.[37]

There is no obligation on an employer to comply with this request. However, such inference as may seem appropriate may be drawn by the Director, the Circuit Court or the Labour Court for the failure to supply the information. Similarly, if the information supplied by an employer is false or misleading.[38]

No victimisation: no dismissal or other penalties for complaint

Dismissal

It is a separate criminal offence under the 1998 Act to dismiss an employee for making a complaint of sexual harassment or harassment in good faith. On conviction for this victimisation, the employee may be subject **either** to an award of compensation (on top of any amount awarded for the earlier

---

[37] Section 76(1), (2) and (3).
[38] Section 81.

act(s) of harassment) **or** to orders of reinstatement or re-engagement. A court fine will also be imposed on conviction and this is irrespective of whether the court makes any order of compensation.[39]

Other penalisation

The 1998 Act also protects employees who seek redress under the Act or give evidence in such proceedings from being victimised *by other penalisation other than dismissal* for so doing either during the proceedings or afterwards.[40]

Compensation awards for victimisation have proved very substantial and will continue to do so.

Employers should be particularly vigilant of this protection and ensure that nothing is said or done, as far as reasonably practicable, that could be interpreted by an employee as victimisation in any way.

What the courts say

As a result, it is of immense importance for employers to be aware of the types of treatment of employees that may lead to claims of victimisation. For example, if there are *genuine redundancies* to be made in the business in a period after any employee has taken a claim or acted as a witness against the employer, that employer must ensure that the selection of that employee for redundancy is scrupulously fair and is capable of being so demonstrated if needs be.

In simple terms, it is also important for employers to know where they can draw the line safely in their dealings with such employees.

There is no definition of the term '*other penalisation*' in the 1998 Act and this comes down to a case-by-case basis.

---

[39] Section 98.

[40] Section 74(2).

Furthermore, the only real guidance provided in the Act is that the victimisation must be *solely or mainly* occasioned by an employee being involved in proceedings against his employer, in one of the ways specified and protected, under the Act.[41] This fails to deal with many of the practical problems that employers may be faced with, in dealing with staff, rosters and the terms and conditions of work not only after the hearing, but also before and during the proceedings themselves when there has not yet even been any adverse finding made against an employer! For small businesses, this is of particular seriousness. However, two important decisions have recently provided further guidance on these points.

In the course of proceedings

Firstly an English House of Lords decision has confirmed that not every instance of adverse treatment or '*penalisation*' arising out of the course of litigation may necessarily be punishable by the courts. The case involved the refusal of an employer to give his employee a reference pending the outcome of proceedings against him. The entitlement of an employer to do this in Ireland is expressly protected under the 1998 Act and this is not why the decision is important.[42] It is important because it is the most recent affirmation by the Law Lords that certain acts taken by an employer solely to preserve his legal position pending the conclusion of litigation may not automatically be considered as 'victimisation.

---

41 *Ibid.*

42 Section 76(4).

Chief Constable of West Yorkshire Police v. Khan.
Victimisation: in search of the missing link?[43]

Judgment

The House of Lords, interpreting the specific definition of 'victimisation' under the UK Race Relations Act 1976, held that:

- Employers ought to be able to take steps to protect their positions in pending discrimination proceedings without laying themselves open to a charge of victimisation.
- A test that is likely, in most cases, to give the right answer is to ask whether the employer would have refused such a request if the litigation had been concluded, whatever the outcome. If the answer is no, then it will usually follow that the reason for the refusal was not to victimise an employee.
- On the other hand, if the fact that an employee had commenced proceedings under the Act was the real reason why he received less favourable treatment, then it is no answer to such a charge that an employer would have behaved in the same way towards some other employee who had never taken a claim against him.

The importance of this decision does not so much depend on the interpretation and application given to the particular piece of English statute but rather on the general principles and *the reasoning* outlined by the House of Lords in deciding what is appropriate conduct in dealing with employees in the course of proceedings. Such principles equally have a bearing on the definition of 'victimisation' in Ireland since, although derived from differing statutory sources and conditions, concrete examples are provided, in cases such as this, as to

---

[43] [2001] I.R.L.R. 830 (December).

the grounds on which conduct may be condemned as penalisation under the Irish 1998 Act.

The lessons?

Actions taken by employers, specifically and solely to protect their legal positions and to avoid prejudicing their case, pending the outcome of such litigation, may not automatically fall within the scope of victimisation. However, this is always going to be a matter of fact to be proved by an employer at the hearing of the substantive claim and further guidance will be required from the courts and industrial tribunals to provide a more complete and certain picture on this point.

Nonetheless, it **always** remains the case that if the motivation of an employer is **to punish** an employee for taking the litigation, any acts on foot of this will be considered as penalties. Moreover, where the employee is merely a witness to proceedings or has given notice of same, as is also protected in the 1998 Act, such arguments could never be successfully relied upon.[44] Similarly, after the proceedings are ended, an employer must ensure to avoid any behaviour or alterations capable of being considered victimisation.

In other words, employers should always avoid putting themselves in the position where any such charge may be made against them. As the next case shows, the consequences of failure are both serious and potentially very expensive.

In The Aftermath of Proceedings

The second case is an Irish determination of an Equality Officer in 2001.

---

[44] Section 74(2)(b) and (c).

McCarthy v. Dublin Corporation. *Sharpening the Blades of Anti-Victimisation!*[45]

Background

The claimant had previously brought a claim of discrimination against her employer, Dublin Corporation, before the Labour Court in December 1996. The claimant, a legal assistant, employed by the respondent had been successful in an earlier sex discrimination action due to their failure to promote her to the post of senior legal assistant. **At first instance, the Equality Officer had identified the following as alleged victimisation:**

- Since the date of the previous claim, her immediate manager, the Chief Clerk, had ignored her for a period of three years from September 24, 1997 until his departure from the employment of the respondent in October 9, 2000.
- The In-house newsletter, 'Forum', distributed widely within the offices of Dublin Corporation had misrepresented the results of the discrimination claim and, despite her written requests to the City Manager, the publication had not been corrected. It was alleged that the Personnel Officer had been responsible for this.
- A subsequent bullying complaint had been made *against her*. The internal investigation into that complaint had been conducted contrary to fair procedures
- and natural justice (see Chapter 5).
- The claimant had been socially isolated at work since she had referred her original claim of discrmination.
- Despite repeated complaints by the claimant about these

[45] [2001] ELR 255. See Determination of the Labour Court on appeal: EDA/022, Chairman Ms Caroline Jenkins, July 2, 2002.

incidents of victimisation, no action was ever taken by the respondents.

Decision

At first instance, the decision found that the claimant had been victimised contrary to the 1998 Act. She was awarded compensation in the amount of £40,000. This decision was appealed to the Labour Court and the amount of the award of compensation was reduced to €25,000. This was because the Labour Court determined that the respondent had not victimised the claimant by deviating from fair procedures. There was one exception: the investigators had gone too far in recommending disciplinary action rather than simply referring the finding of the investigation to the personnel officer.

On this point, the Court simply ordered that the disciplinary hearing be heard on a *de novo* basis. Moreover, the Labour Court upheld the entitlement of the personnel officer to decide on disciplinary action as an appropriate function. Therefore, it rejected entirely any suggestion that his involvement in the process was an act of penalisation or victimisation of the claimant simply because of the claim of an alleged misprepresentation by that Officer of the earlier proceedings in 'Forum'.

Some Important Conclusions

Both the Equality Officer and the Labour Court concluded that the effect of victimisation is to undermine the entire purpose and effectiveness of the legislation and is completely unacceptable. Therefore, it will always be dealt with severely.

The Equality Officer concluded that the mere adoption of a policy was insufficient unless it was brought to the attention of staff and a consciousness was created in all employees as to what consituted discrimination. This means that simply adopting an anti-harassment policy across the nine grounds will not be enough for an employer in order to meet his statutory obligations. The Labour Court backed up this conclusion.

Finally, what is interesting and of much importance is the fact that both the Equality Officer and the Labour Court expressly applied the common law test of vicarious liability as well as the 1998 Act directly to the instances of victimisation complained of in holding the respondent employer responsible. Both had to be applied simply because many of the instances of victimisation complained of related to periods prior to the introduction of the 1998 Act, which creates the automatic or 'strict' liability of employers for offences. However, the Equality Officer and the Labour Court had no difficulty in holding that acts like victimisation may be carried out within the scope of employment.

- The respondent was vicariously liable both at common law and under statute for the victimisation of the claimant as a result of the Chief Clerk refusing to speak to her.
- The respondent was vicariously liable at common law for the inaccurate reporting at management meeting and the publication afterwards of the decision of her earlier discrimination claim and for the failure to correct the error. In so doing, those involved had acted within the scope of their employment.

As such, having considered the scope, nature and importance of the legal protection provided by the rules against harassment and sexual harassment in this chapter and against bullying earlier in Chapter 3, the next chapter will deal with the practical implications and pitfalls of putting such protection into operation and, more importantly, applying them in reality.

Chapter 5

Stamping Out Bullying and Harassment At Work: The Vital Policy and Procedure

General Overview

The basics

As with stress, when it comes to bullying and harassment, prevention is better than cure. Therefore, employers should adopt, implement and monitor a comprehensive, effective and accessible policy on workplace bullying, sexual harassment and harassment. The policy dealing with the prevention of workplace bullying and harassment should be produced following consultation with the safety and employee representatives. A policy is most likely to be effective when it is jointly agreed between the employees or their representatives and the employer, as a shared sense of responsibility is important in the development of anti-bullying/harassment culture.[1]

The policy and complaints procedure should also, where appropriate and as far as reasonably practicable, be adopted after consultation and negotiation with clients, customers and other business contacts or their representatives about its contents and implementation.

It should be written, dated and signed by the employer or his senior management (depending on the size of the business)

---

[1] Section 13 of the Safety, Health and Welfare at Work Act 1989 also provides that consultation in this way is a statutory duty.

and updated when appropriate. The language used in the Policy should be simple and direct. It should be accessible to employees with literacy problems and to those who do not speak fluent English.

It should be made available to all staff and highlighted as part of the induction process. It should also be publicised among existing staff on an ongoing basis. Reference should also be made to the Anti-Bullying/Harassment Policy in the Safety Statement.

Guidance on the Preparation of the Policy

The Anti-Bullying/Harassment Policy must incorporate the following terms in order for it to be considered effective.[2]

The core elements and implementation steps

1. The policy should begin by declaring

(a) The commitment of the business to ensuring that the workplace is free from bullying, sexual harassment and harassment.

(b) That all employees have a right to be treated with dignity and respect.

(c) That complaints by employees will be treated with fairness and sensitivity and in as confidential a manner as is consistent with a fair investigation.

---

2 *FACTS*, European Agency For Safety and Health at Work, Fact sheet, no.23, Belgium 2002; *Code of Practice on Sexual Harassment and Harassment At Work*, Equality Authority, Dublin 2002 (as effected by S.I. No. 78 of 2002); *Code of Practice on the Prevention of Workplace Bullying*, H.S.A., Dublin, 2002.

(d) That, in the event of a complaint of bullying, sexual harassment/harassment being upheld against employees, that the disciplinary process will be invoked that may include disciplinary action up to and including dismissal. In the event of a complaint being upheld against non-employees, appropriate sanctions may be imposed which could, in particular circumstances, include the termination of contracts, suspension of service or an exclusion from the premises as appropriate.

(f) That using the Complaints Procedure does not affect the Complainant's statutory rights to make a complaint under the Industrial Relations mechanisms and it should specify the statutory time limits.

(g) That in the course of investigating any complaints of a breach of the Policy, the employer will make no assumptions about the guilt of the alleged harasser.

(h) That, in the adoption and in the implementation of the Policy, all due regard is accorded to developments in best practice and, in particular, the:

Code of Practice on the Prevention of Workplace Bullying (2002);

Code of Practice on Sexual Harassment and Harassment in the Workplace (2002);

Code of Practice Detailing Procedures for Addressing Bullying in the Workplace (2002).

2. Definition

(a) The Policy should set out the definitions of bullying, sexual harassment and harassment that are simple, clear and practical. In particular, it should clarify that

- A claim for harassment must be based on one of nine specified grounds whereas bullying can include any inappropriate behaviour that may reasonably be regarded as an affront to dignity.

- Acts of bullying not linked to one of the nine grounds is not covered by the Employment Equality Act 1998.
- An isolated, once-off incident of inappropriate behaviour, although an affront to dignity, is not considered bullying for the purposes of a valid complaint, whereas a single act of unwelcome behaviour may constitute a valid complaint of sexual harassment/harassment.

(b) A non-exhaustive list of examples should be provided. (A number of such examples have been provided in earlier chapters).

(c) The Policy should state that the protection extends to:

- Bullying, sexual harassment/harassment by co-workers, clients, customers and other business contacts;
- Beyond the workplace to conferences and training and may extend to work related social events;
- Different treatment of an employee because he/she has rejected or accepted the sexual harassment/harassment;
- In the case of sexual harassment/harassment, employment agencies and vocational training.

(d) The Policy should emphasise that it is up to an employee to decide what is unwelcome or offensive behaviour, irrespective of the attitude of others.

(e) The Policy should state that employees who make a complaint or who give evidence in proceedings will not be victimised.

3. Allocation of responsibilities under the Act

The Policy should state that management and others in positions of authority have a particular responsibility to ensure that bullying, sexual harassment/harassment does not occur and that complaints are addressed speedily. The Policy should state that, in particular, management should:

(a) Provide good example by treating all in the workplace with courtesy and respect;

(b) Promote awareness of the business policy and complaints procedure;

(c) Be vigilant for signs of bullying and harassment and take action before a problem escalates;

(d) Respond sensitively to an employee who makes a complaint of bullying or harassment;

(e) Explain the procedures to be followed if a complaint is made;

(f) Ensure that an employee making a complaint is not victimised for doing so;

(g) Monitor and follow up a situation after a complaint is made so that the bullying, sexual harassment/harassment does not recur.

4. Trade unions

The Policy should address the contribution to be made by the trade union(s). Trade Unions play an important role in prevention and in providing information, advice and representation to both the employees who have made a complaint and to the employees against whom a complaint is made.

5. Employees

The Policy should make it clear that employees can contribute to achieving a bullying and sexual harassment/harassment free environment through cooperating with management and trade union strategies to eliminate bullying and harassment. It must also make clear that bullying and sexual harassment/harassment by employees constitutes misconduct and may lead to disciplinary action.

6. Non-employees

The Policy should point out that bullying, sexual harassment and harassment by non-employees such as clients, contractors and other business contacts will not be tolerated and may lead to the termination/non-renewal of contracts, the suspension/non-renewal of services, exclusion from the premises or the imposition of other appropriate sanctions (depending on the circumstances of the business).

7. Communication of the policy

The Policy should include a commitment to its effective communication. It should be communicated effectively to all those potentially affected by it, in particular, management, workers, customers, contractors and business contacts including those who supply and receive goods and services.

This effective means of communication should include: newsletters, training manuals, training courses, leaflet drops, websites, e-mails, notice boards and staff meetings.

To employees

Employees, including those in management and all other positions of responsibility, should be made aware of the Policy as part of any formal induction process to their new job and working environment along with the other health and safety rules and regulations.

Employers are advised to consider a staff handbook where reasonably practicable to be distributed to all employees as part of the induction process. Such a handbook should be kept under on-going review to reflect developments.

To non-employees

No on-going relationship

There may be practical difficulties in ensuring that the policy is effectively communicated to every relevant non-employee particularly where there is no on-going relationship with the business. However, it is advised that summaries of policies should be displayed prominently in the workplace to which these non-employees have access. This should contain a short statement confirming the policies existence and the business' commitment to it. It should also state that the complete policy is available on request. This type of approach is appropriate to alert the general public of the policy as they avail of certain types of general services from the business. For example, public houses or restaurants.

On-going relationship

Where there is an on-going relationship with customers and clients, the effective communication of the policy is easier to achieve. A number of means may promote this aim:

- Leaflets summarising the policy being prominently displayed in areas where members of the public, clients and customers attend such as receptions and waiting rooms.
- Include a leaflet or short written summary of the Policy in any of the business brochures.

- It may even be appropriate for the contracts of the employer with customers, contractors or other business contacts to expressly include a term providing that the bullying, sexual harassment/harassment of the employees of the employer will constitute a repudiation of the contract and may be a ground for the employer to terminate the contract.

It has been the tradition of the courts to imply terms into private contracts by analogy with statutes applicable in the same area. Similarly, in the future, in any contractual dispute on this basis, it may also be the case that the courts will imply such a term into all relevant contracts by analogy with the statutory duties of employers now under the 1998 Act.[3]

8. Monitoring

The Policy should incorporate a commitment to monitoring incidents of bullying and sexual harassment/harassment. This is particularly important in the context of an employer seeking to minimise his legal exposure to litigation. The only way that a business can know if its policy and procedure are working is to keep careful track of all complaints of bullying and sexual harassment/harassment and how and when they are resolved. The monitoring information should be used to evaluate the policy and procedures at regular intervals with alterations and improvements made if there is some weakness identified in the system.

9. Training

The Policy should contain a commitment to train all staff on issues of bullying and sexual harassment/harassment.

An important means of ensuring that bullying and

---

[3] McMahon and Binchy, *The Law of Torts*, 3rd Edition, (Butterworths, Dublin, 2000), p.488.

harassment does not occur is through the provision of training for managers, supervisors and all staff. This should happen for staff at induction or through appropriate awareness raising initiatives.

Such training should aim to **identify** the factors that contribute to a workplace free of bullying and harassment, to **familiarise** participants with their responsibilities and to **inform** them of any problems they are likely to encounter under the Policy e.g. the meaning of the words 'unwelcome' or 'reasonably be regarded.'

10. The complaints procedure

The Policy should set out a complaints procedure. This should be attached to the policy. Clients, contractors or business contacts who interact on a frequent basis with the business should be made aware of the employees' right to make a complaint and that they may be requested to participate in the process. See below.

11. Reviews

The Policy should include a commitment to review it on a regular basis in lines with changes in statute, case law or other developments. A competent person should be designated to ensure that such monitoring, training and reviews occur.

12. Victimisation

The Policy should guarantee that an employee invoking the complaints procedure will not be victimised or subject to sanction for making a complaint in good faith, for giving evidence in proceedings arising out of it or for giving notice to do so. The effective implementation of an Anti-Bullying/ Harassment Policy requires a reprisal free environment.

13. Counselling Services

The Policy should include details as to any counselling and support services available for victims and perpetrators and how to contact them. This information should also come with the assurance of absolute privacy and confidentiality.

The Anti-bullying/harassment policy should be incorporated as a part of the contract of employment of each employee.

The Complaint's Procedure

Are you Keeping up with the Latest Best Practice?

As discussed earlier, since March 2002, new, formal, streamlined procedures have been introduced and recommended by the relevant State agencies for implementation with the purpose of addressing bullying and harassment in the workplace. Moreover, they have legal status and are admissible in court. Indeed, in deciding sexual harassment/harassment claims, a court or tribunal must take into account the Code of Practice on Harassment if it is relevant to any issue before it. Therefore, it is vital that employers are aware of the procedures recommended under these Codes and as far as possible adopt and implement them as part of their own anti-bullying/harassment system at work.

Moreover, for those many employers who may already have anti-bullying/harassment procedures in place, it is also important that existing procedures are kept under on-going review to ensure their adequacy and effective implementation. Therefore, it may be worthwhile to test the adequacy of any existing procedures by now comparing them with those recommended in this chapter. It is important that employers be aware that not only is it good practice for them to implement and keep up to date with these procedures, as already discussed, it is also an important factor in determining their exposure to compensation claims in any future litigation. The effective incorporation and implementation of the new procedures will be a factor to which a court or tribunal will, in the future, have serious regard in the event of any claim against an employer.

The **Codes of Practice of 2002** provide for a double-layered procedure. There is the informal procedure and the formal procedure.

Informal procedure

On many occasions, the recipient of bullying or harassment simply wants it to stop thereby allowing him or her to get on with the job. As such, an informal approach may be the better way to resolve an issue of bullying or harassment in the workplace in the first instance. It is always beneficial to attempt to find a non-confrontational solution before undertaking the formal, more legalistic route. After all, the smaller the workforce, the closer the inter-relationship between all the parties in the workplace and the more likely it is that the parties concerned may have to work together again there. It also minimises the conflict, stress and distress to which a complainant may be already subject.

> **A**. Any employee who feels that he is being bullied or harassed should object to the conduct where this is possible and appropriate. In many cases, this may be sufficient. He should explain **clearly** to the alleged perpetrator(s) engaging in the unwelcome or offensive behaviour in question that it is unwelcome or that it offends him and that it interferes with his work.
>
> In circumstances, where the employee finds it difficult to approach the alleged perpetrator(s) directly, he should seek help and advice, on a strictly confidential basis, from **a contact person**. A contact person could be one of the following:

- A supervisor or line manager;
- Any manager in the workplace;
- Human resource/personnel officer;
- Another employee/trade union representative.

In this situation, it is advised that the contact person listen patiently, be supportive and discuss the various options open to an employee.

B. Having consulted with the contact person, the complainant may request the assistance of the contact person **in raising the issue** with the alleged perpetrator(s). In this situation, the approach of the contact person should be by way of a non-confrontational, calm, confidential discussion with a view to resolving the issue in an informal, low-key manner.

C. However, a complainant employee may decide, and is entitled, to bypass, for whatever reason, this informal approach. **Choosing not to use the informal procedure should not reflect negatively on a complainant during the formal process.**

NOTE: It is important for employers, line managers and HR personnel to note the simple point that they themselves, if they become aware of a problem or when they receive a complaint, should not 'jump the gun' for whatever reason and institute the formal procedure without *giving the complainant* him/herself the full opportunity to choose. Employers moving straight into a formal procedure when the complainant may have been satisfied by an informal approach may actually constitute a ground of bullying or victimisation of the alleged bully by the employer!

The formal procedure

If an employee believes that an informal approach is inappropriate, if the bullying or harassment is too serious for informality or if, after the informal stage, the bullying persists or recommences, the formal procedures should be invoked. Under this Procedure:

Part One: The making and receipt of the complaint

A. The complainant should make a formal complaint in writing to his or her immediate supervisor, or if preferred, any member of management. The complaint should be confined to precise details of the actual incidents of bullying.

B. The alleged perpetrators should be notified in writing that an allegation of bullying has been made against him or her. He or she should be given a copy of the complainant's statement and advised that he or she shall be afforded a fair opportunity to respond to the allegation(s).

C. The complainant should be subject to an initial examination by a designated member of management who is considered impartial with a view to determining an appropriate course of action.

An example of an appropriate course of action at this stage might be exploring the acceptability of a mediated solution or a view that the issue might still be resolved informally.

Should either of these approaches be deemed inappropriate or inconclusive, **a formal investigation of the complaint should take place** with a view to determining the facts and the credibility or otherwise of the allegation(s).

REMEMBER: The role must be taken extremely seriously and always bear in mind **the implications** this investigation will have on the jobs, reputations and livelihood of both the complainant and the alleged bully or harasser. In many cases, not only will the employer need general guidelines such as these but also, he himself, will need to obtain **specific legal advice** on his role in the particular situation. What is required in any particular instance will depend on the circumstances and/or the complexity of the case and this may require the adaption of the procedure. In simple terms, an employer not only needs to have his or her procedure, he or she also needs to get it right in each case! If not, the employer may make matters worse and find himself directly exposed and in the firing line. This issue is discussed in more detail later in this chapter.

Part Two: The investigation

D. The investigation should be conducted by either a designated member(s) of management or, if deemed, appropriate, an agreed third party.

It is suggested that at least two people should investigate a complaint with a gender balance and diversity across the other eight grounds in the 1998 Act. However, it is accepted that this may be impractical on occasion.

Nevertheless, in all circumstances, the investigation should be conducted thoroughly, sensitively, utmost confidentiality and good faith and with due regard to the rights of both the complainant and the alleged perpetrator(s). The investigation should be, and perceived to be, independent and objective. Those conducting it should not be connected with the allegations in any way.

E. The investigation should be governed by terms of reference, preferably agreed between the parties, or their legal advisers, in advance. The terms of reference must always include the following;

- What this formal procedure provided here involves and the relevant time limits (if not agreed).
- That both parties have the right to be accompanied and/or represented.
- That the alleged perpetrator(s) is to be given full details in writing not only of the nature of the complaint but also all other relevant written statements and any other documentation or evidence including witness statements, interview notes or records of meetings held with the complainant and witnesses relating to the complaint.
- That the alleged perpetrator will be given reasonable time to consider the documentation and an opportunity to respond.
- That the alleged perpetrator(s) is or is not being afforded a full oral hearing in order to cross-examine the complainant and, if so, the date, location and procedure for same.

F. The investigator(s) should then meet with the complainant and the alleged perpetrator(s) and any witnesses or relevant persons on a one-to-one confidential basis with a view to establishing the facts surrounding the allegations. Both the complainant and the alleged perpetrator(s) may, at this point, be accompanied by a legal representative or a work colleague or an employee/trade union representative, if so requested.

G. Every effort should be made to carry out and complete the investigation as quickly as possible and preferably within an agreed time frame. On completion of the investigation, having duly considered all the evidence and representations submitted, the investigator(s) should produce a written report for management containing the findings of the investigation.

H. The complainant and alleged perpetrator(s) should be informed of the findings of the investigation.

I. Both parties should be given the opportunity to comment on the findings before any action is decided upon by the employer or management. Such comments should be duly considered.

Part Three: The outcome

J. Should management decide that the complaint is well founded against an employee, it will be necessary to decide whether the disciplinary procedures of the business should be invoked. The perpetrator should be given a formal interview to determine an appropriate course of action. Such action could involve, as an example, counselling and monitoring or the bringing of the issue through the disciplinary and grievance procedure of the employment.

K. Should management decide that the complaint is well founded against a non-employee, it will be necessary to decide what sanctions to enforce against him or his employer. This could extend, appropriate, to:

- The exclusion of the individual from the premises;
- The suspension or termination of a contract with him;

- The suspension or termination of a service supplied by or to him.

L. The management decision may also, or as an alternative, recommend other actions such as the more effective promotion of the business policy on bullying, sexual harassment/harassment or training.

If a right of appeal exists both parties should be informed of it and the time limits and procedure involved. If either party is unhappy with the outcome of the investigation, the issue may be processed through the normal industrial relations mechanisms.

Non-employees

It is probable that if the person accused of the bullying or sexual harassment/harassment is not an employee, he or she will not wish to participate in the formal procedure and, thereby, it will not be possible to secure their participation.

Nonetheless, a non-employee must be kept informed of all developments and given the opportunity to respond to them. The outcome of the investigation and any potential sanctions must also be explained to the non-employee and/ or any person or company for whom he/she works.

Confidentiality

All individuals involved in the procedures should maintain confidentiality on the subject.

Training and Awareness Raising

The Health and Safety Authority considers that all personnel with a role in both the formal and informal procedures should be made aware of the appropriate policies and procedures and should, if possible, include appropriate training. An example of such relevant persons would be:

- Designated members of management;
- Worker representatives;
- 'Contact persons';
- Union representatives.

However, an employer should consider which other persons may be considered for such treatment in his or her workplace.

Furthermore, as with the Policy, the Anti-Bullying/ Harassment Procedure should be incorporated as an express term of the contract of employment to which all employees and the employer must agree, including the specified penalties, suspensions (with or without pay) and other possible sanctions that may arise from a finding of wrongdoing up to and including dismissal.

The Codes of 2002: No exercise in window dressing, they mean business!

Finally, any notion that the new Codes of Practice or the recommendations and warnings they contain, as outlined in the course of this chapter, are merely another exercise in window dressing or another strand of red tape should be dispelled immediately. This may be especially so for employers and HR personnel concerned with established policies and procedures in their business or organisation. These Codes signify a real and fundamental vigour now being brought to bear on the area of employer liability arising out of stress, bullying and harassment in the workplace. Indeed, these claims may have already passed a milestone, since the charmed status accorded to the Codes has been unquestionably confirmed by the E.A.T in a determination in 2002. Therefore, before best practice for complaints procedures is considered in more detail, it is necessary to highlight, on the basis of this determination, what not to do.

Browne v. Ventelo Telecommunications (Ireland) Limited. You break the code, you pay the price![4]

Background

The claimant's problems began with the respondent in January 1999. In or around July 1999, the claimant began experiencing sexual harassment of an explicit nature from a senior manager in the organisation. This behaviour occurred over a period of months and on numerous occasions. This situation was made particularly severe as the Human Resource Manager of the respondent was also actually implicated in the unlawful activities. As a result, the claimant employee made a complained to the Managing Director of the respondent. She was requested to put her complaint in writing and she duly did so. Thereafter, a formal complaints procedure under the internal Human Resource Manual was invoked. The complaint was substantiated and she received a letter from the respondent acknowledging that her complaint was well founded. However, the respondent was willing to accept an apology from the particular harassing manager in question. As such, the claimant received a written apology from that individual. She was asked to sign a letter agreeing to waive her entitlement to pursue further legal proceedings arising out of the matter. She refused. Thereafter, she alleged that she was subjected to a campaign of bullying, harassment and intimidation that ultimately left her with no option but to resign. In this way, she pursued a claim for constructive dismissal through the EAT under the unfair dismissals legislation.[5]

---

4 UD 597/2001. EAT: July 16, 2002.

5 Unfair Dismissal Acts 1977 to 1993.

A Summary of the behaviour

Sexual harassment: The initial complaint concerned sexual harassment comprising of lewd comments and other spoken words of an explicitly sexual, unwelcome and offensive nature. The conduct also comprised physical gestures and expressions of a sexual, unwelcome and offensive nature.

Complaints made against the claimant: Following this episode, her relationship deteriorated with the HR Manager. Meetings were held and official complaints were lodged by an Administrator and a work-colleague claiming she was uncooperative. Prior to this, there had never been complaints about her. The HR manager told her on a regular basis that she was rude on the telephone to clients. When the claimant asked for specific examples of this, she was not given any. But she was told that her employer 'was keeping an eye on her'.

Demotion and role conflict: Following the making of the complaint and the claimant's refusal, thereafter, to waive her legal and statutory rights to pursue the matter further, her job and role specification was altered to the extent that it was she alleged, in reality, a demotion. When she returned from a holiday, she noticed that a colleague, who had been her junior and who she had helped to train in, had been allocated tasks that had previously been done by her. When she questioned that person about this, the claimant was told that the matter could not be discussed with her. In fact, the junior colleague had been promoted to Personal Assistant to a manager in the company at the start of January 2000 and had been told not to tell the claimant until the end of that month when the promotion was formalised. The claimant's role and job description had been seriously and definitely compressed.

When she received a new job specification, the claimant also discovered that certain tasks had been removed from it in circumstances where she had never received any complaints about her work in those areas at all. The reasons for their removal were unclear and never properly clarified by a formal explanation. The claimant and her promoted colleague remained working together in a close environment. However, as a result of this change in job specification and the manner in which it was handled, the relationship between them was difficult and deteriorated.

The excessive scrutiny of the claimant: Evidence was also given at the hearing of the action that the claimant was 'being called upstairs for the slightest thing and would come back crying'. Evidence was further given that the HR Manager had been provoking or orchestrating a situation whereby the claimant's work colleague had been encouraged to formally complain about her. On January 17, 2000, an e-mail had been sent to the HR Manager by that colleague listing ongoing difficulties that she was experiencing with the claimant. She wanted to clarify their roles. Indeed, she also felt that the claimant was confrontational, aggressive and behaving as a bully. However, this employee also said that this e-mail was only intended as an agenda for a meeting on the issue and not as a complaint about the claimant. Nevertheless, the HR Manager, on his own initiative, typed up the e-mail into a letter and had the work colleague sign this document. A meeting was then held with the General Manager of the respondent in which these issues were raised.

At the hearing before the EAT, this employee confirmed that she was not aware that, at the time, her e-mail or the letter she signed would be used as a warning to the claimant. Most sinister of all, this work colleague gave evidence that this HR Manager had wanted her to formally complain when she did not want to. This employee told the EAT that the HR Manager said that a formal complaint was necessary so that they could 'get her out of the company'.

The claimant, herself, had made a formal complaint in

writing about this conduct to the same General Manager. However, she was told that she did not have the required evidence and her complaint was dropped.

The disciplining of the claimant: A disciplinary hearing was held on September 28, 2000 where issues were raised as to the claimant's performance and her level of absenteeism. At this point, she was taking a lot of sick days due to the onset of work-related stress. Another disciplinary meeting was held on October 27, 2000 where her absenteeism was again discussed. At another meeting on November 2, 2000, the claimant pointed out that she was unhappy with her job specification and that she was now being asked to do tasks which she had not done since starting to work for the company. On November 15, 2000, yet another meeting was held in which she was told that a final written warning would be issued to her. This duly appeared and was dated November 23.

Absence of representation: The internal Human Resource Manual of the respondent provided that a nominated representative may be brought along to such disciplinary hearings and this person could be a colleague *or some other person chosen* by an employee. However, in her case, the claimant only received the notice for the disciplinary hearing of September 28 on the same day! In this notice, moreover, her right to representation referred only to bringing *a colleague*. Not only did this leave her with little opportunity to either prepare herself or secure representation for the meeting, by referring only to a colleague, it had also departed for no reason from the procedures in place. In a further departure from the internal procedure, the claimant had to notify the respondent with the identity of this colleague in advance. Finally, when the claimant requested that a solicitor represent her at another meeting, she was refused notwithstanding the internal Manual.

Towards the end of November 2000, there were still ongoing issues concerning her job performance, however, no further disciplinary action was taken against her. Nevertheless, at this point, the claimant felt that she had no other option but to hand in her notice and terminate her employment. She resigned on February 28, 2001 without giving her reasons for leaving.

Determination

On the basis of the evidence before it, the Tribunal identified, isolated and condemned each and every one of the acts listed above. As a result of this litany of hostility, it determined that, the Claimant had, in fact, been constructively dismissed. She was awarded £10,000 or €12,697.38 in compensation for that unfair dismissal.

In so doing, it also formulated a new and interesting concept in its thinking about the types of behaviour it labels as bullying and harassment. This concept is entitled "cosmetic bullying". In much the same way as discrimination can be indirect in that, although couched in neutral and objective terms, the intent and design of certain decisions and behaviour may be to inordinately disadvantage one employee or group of employees over another. Similarly, the Tribunal defined cosmetic bullying as conduct inherent in the faulty dynamics of the employment relationship arising out of the *creation* of a systematic problem of conflict *designed* to humiliate the victim. As such, no matter what 'designer label', as the Tribunal called it, an employer uses, whether it is the changing of job specifications, formal warnings, the disciplinary procedures or the restructuring of offices or of line management, it will look at all the circumstances of the case to see if the actual motivation is to inflict harassment, bullying or victimisation on an employee. In particular, in this case, the promotion of the work colleague was done in secret and *sub rosa* and the respondent never denied this. As a result, the Tribunal concluded that the bullying techniques of the respondent:

> "result in the low self-esteem of the employee and, accordingly, will embitter employees [against each other] and fuel hostility in the workplace."

In this case, it determined that the motivation of the respondent in its conduct was to show the claimant 'who is boss'. Moreover, for the Tribunal, the bullying and harassment was all the more odious because it involved the HR manager, the very person an employee should be able to rely on in such a situation. Finally, it is a good example of a determination that understands the relationship between bullying and the use and abuse of fair procedures as a weapon of control by an employer.

Therefore, the Tribunal is keenly aware of opportunities for bullying and harassment available to an employer through the manipulation of otherwise neutral structures, policies and procedures of the workplace.

Calculation of compensation

In so doing, the Tribunal accepted the fact that the claimant had only been out of work for a *one-month* period and that her financial loss attributable to the dismissal was relatively small. Nevertheless, the Tribunal equally relied on the fact that financial loss includes not just actual loss but also any estimated prospective loss of income attributable to that dismissal. Therefore, the Tribunal decided that, in the present case, it ***must*** have regard to the terms of the respective Codes of Practice and, in particular, the *Code of Practice on Sexual Harassment and Harassment At Work*. Therefore, in arriving at its conclusion on this basis, the following factors were relied on.

- The claimant was very distressed by the behaviour of her employer and was still coming to terms with it.
- An employee suffers short and long-term damage as a result of sexual harassment. On this point, the Tribunal relied on the *Code of Practice on Sexual Harassment and Harassment at Work.*
- Therefore, the claimant may not have fully come to terms with the conduct of her employer and there is a possibility that she may incur a loss or diminution of her earnings as a result of the nature of the constructive dismissal.
- Since her actual loss was small, her prospective loss, because of any long-term damage may be greater. Therefore, the amount of compensation was measured in accordance with what was just and equitable in all the circumstances.

Lessons?

Firstly, it is interesting that the EAT chose to rely on the sexual harassment ground as the basis for awarding compensation for the dismissal. As pointed out in Chapter 4, dismissal claims (including constructive dismissal) arising out of unlawful conduct, such as sexual harassment, under the 1998 Act are heard exclusively by the Labour Court or, where appropriate, the Circuit Court. However, this jurisdiction exclusion is viewed narrowly here since the EAT had no difficulty awarding compensation on the basis of the effects of sexual harassment. Therefore, it appears that, where a constructive dismissal complaint is based on a number of grounds, some of which are also acts of sexual harassment or harassment, then that claim may, nevertheless, still be brought to the EAT under the unfair dismissals legislation rather than to the Labour Court under the employment equality regime. However, it may be recalled that an employee cannot pursue both.

Secondly, like *Allen* in Chapter 3, this also expands the boundaries of the approach now taken for compensating future financial loss attributable to dismissal. However, it goes even further than *Allen*. In this case, Ms Browne, unlike Ms Allen, had found new employment and returned to work within one month of resigning. It was also not suggested that she was unfit to return to work. On the other hand, Ms Allen was compensated for loss of future earnings arising out of actual stress-related illness suffered and that complicated her return to the workforce. Moreover, the test in Allen requires an employee to show an actual stress-related illness since, in order to recover compensation, Ms Allen had to show her illness was because of and connected to the bullying and harassment at issue. This involved diagnosis. No formal diagnosis was required in *Browne*.

In simple terms, whereas the basis of the compensation in *Allen* was actual damage to health, the basis for compensation in *Browne* is potential or *latent* damage.

This was made possible expressly by the Tribunal's reliance on and application of the best practice and guidance introduced by the *Code of Conduct*. Instead of requiring medical diagnosis, the guidance of the Code sufficed. This is the final innovation of this determination.

Whatever about the practical application of this approach into the future, it now has real and serious implications for the financial exposure of employers to such claims. Policies and procedures incorporating most recent legal and health and safety development must be introduced or incorporated into existing procedures. If needs be, legal and HR advice may facilitate this process. Once this is done, procedures should be adhered to rigidly. How to deal with such realities is the topic considered in the next section.

Applying the Procedure: Know the Pitfalls! Investigations and the Duty to be Fair

How do I keep everyone happy?

Even with the best will in the world, an employer can fall foul of the law if he or she applies the Anti-Bullying and Harassment Procedure incompletely or inadequately. Therefore, the fundamental principle in investigating a complaint of bullying or harassment in the workplace is the need to be as painstaking and even-handed as possible in according fairness to both sides in the inquiry. In short, an employer must ensure that the system is both fair and is seen to be fair. However, in practice, this is often a case of 'easier said than done'. Therefore, it is important for employers to be aware of some basic pitfalls.

The first thing to bear in mind is that this is not just a matter of private contract between an employer and employee, it is a fundamental public right guaranteed by the Constitution of Ireland. As part of that guarantee, two fundamental rights of any fair procedure may be highlighted:

- *Nemo Iudex In Causa Sua*: (The Rule Against The Actual or Perceived Bias of An Adjudicator);
- *Audi Alterem Partem*: (The Rule Requiring the Fair Hearing of Both Parties To A Dispute).

There is no surer a way for an employer ending up in the High Court, whether it be for an application for judicial review or for an injunction to prevent an inquiry, than for failing to apply fair procedures in a given case. This is usually known as a breach of '*constitutional and natural justice*.'

Glover v. BLN Ltd: Falling foul of fairness?[6]

In this important Irish case, the plaintiff employee was neither *told* of the charges against him nor given any *opportunity to deal* with them before his employer arrived at its decision. Mr Justice Walsh of the Supreme Court stated:

- It was necessarily an **implied term** of a contract of employment that an inquiry should be fairly conducted;
- Public policy and constitutional justice require that agreements setting up machinery for taking decisions that may affect rights or impose liabilities should be **interpreted as providing fair procedures;**
- Failure to allow an employee to **meet the charges** against him and to afford him an adequate opportunity **to answer them** is a violation of the obligation to proceed fairly.

It was also decided in a later case that these principles applied to all employees, whether private or public sector, and without regard to their status.[7]

What this means, in practice, is that it now appears to be settled law in Ireland that, *at the very least*, an employee is entitled to be:

- Informed of the charge against him or her;
- Given an opportunity to answer it;
- Given an opportunity to make submissions.[8]

As already seen, the Codes of Practice embody these legal and constitutional requirements in their framework. However,

---

6 [1973] I.R. 388.

7 *Gunn v. B.C.N.E.D* [1990] 2 I.R. 168.

8 *Mooney v. An Post* [1998] E.L.R. 238. Also, Smith, M., '*Workplace Bullying: Internal Investigations and Fair Procedures*, The Bar Review, June/July 2002.

it is the employer who must ultimately put flesh on them. Therefore, the following considerations are vital.

The charge

The employer must not only furnish the employee with the documentation grounding the charge precisely but with all the other information upon which he is relying or may rely in arriving at a decision. An adjudicator must not act on the basis of information that he has not disclosed and furnished to the employee.[9] This is the case even if the consequence of the decision may not ultimately be dismissal but rather damage to the reputation and good name of an employee.[10] One further important point to remember is that the persons ultimately designated with investigating a complaint must have no part in the actual preparation, formulation or drafting of the charge to be relied on by the complainant and furnished to the accused employee. This may appear a very basic point, but, in fact, has resulted in very costly findings being made against employers in recent years in Ireland.

Answering the charge and making submissions

An employee may answer a charge and make submissions by meeting with his employer on a one–to-one basis ('an inquisitorial approach') or he may wish to have an oral hearing with both parties present and an opportunity either himself or through a representative to test by cross-examination the evidence of the complainant against him.

---

9 *Georgopolus v. Beaumont Hospital Board* [1998] 3 I.R. 132, (Supreme Court).

10 *Donner v. Garda Síochána Complaints Board and Anor.* August 14, 2000, per Finnegan J., High Court; Smith M, 'Workplace Bullying: Internal Investigations and Fair Procedures,' *Bar Review*, June/July 2002, p.273.

Representation of the accused employee

In any interview or investigative hearing of a charge (and any disciplinary hearing), the representation accorded to an employee must be effective. The right to be represented must be made known to the employee at the time such a hearing or meeting is proposed. Accordingly, it is necessary to record in writing the terms in which the entitlement was brought to the notice of the employee and his or her actual response to it. If a meeting takes place without the presence of representation, a heavy burden will rest upon the employer to demonstrate that the employee knowingly and intelligently waived his entitlement and that such entitlement was real and effective in the first place. In such a claim, this is not an insurmountable burden for an employer. However, it will be necessary to ensure that the entitlement to representation was in fact a reality and, therefore, was scrupulously respected in order to show a court or tribunal that fairness was observed at the interview stage.[11]

However, an employee is not entitled, automatically, to a formal, quasi-judicial, more complex oral hearing including a right of cross-examination of the complainant and his or her evidence. Whether it is appropriate to grant him or her one will depend on the particular circumstances of the charge.

Three important circumstances determine whether an oral hearing should be granted:

- The seriousness of the allegation against the employee or the importance of his rights in issue as they relate to his continuing tenure of employment, his good name and to his livelihood.[12]

---

[11] *Browne v. Ventelo Telecommunications (Irl) Limited,* UD 597/2001, July 16, 2002.

[12] *Gallagher v. The Revenue Commissioners* [1995] E.L.R. 108.

- The extent to which there is a dispute of the facts between the parties[13]
- Is the complainant in a position to give evidence? A complainant who has been subject to serious bullying may already be in a vulnerable and fragile state mentally and emotionally. Therefore, it may not be appropriate to allow his or her bully or a representative to confront the complainant in the adversarial context of a cross-examination at an oral hearing. This may, in fact, exacerbate the situation. In such a case, the employer may be justified in refusing to allow a confrontation to occur.[14]

In a case where an oral hearing may otherwise be appropriate, is there credible evidence that such a confrontation may so seriously damage the mental health of the victim that it outweighs the risk that injustice may be done to an accused employee? Suspicion that a complainant may be exaggerating symptoms in order to escape being cross-examined could be avoided by requesting that a further psychiatric validation exercise be performed by a psychiatrist or psychologist nominated by the legal representatives of the accused employee. This approach has been accepted by the High Court in Ireland.

However, such an examination would be required to have the prior agreement of the complainant's doctor and to take place in his or her presence.[15]

In circumstances where an employer is unsure as to what side of the threshold a potentially serious charge against an employee may fall, it may be preferable to allow an oral

---

[13] *Gallagher v. The Revenue Commissioners* [1995] E.L.R. 108; *Galvin v. Chief Appeals Officer* [1997] 3 I.R. 240; *Sheriff v. Corrigan* [1999] E.L.R. 146.

[14] *A Worker v. A Hospital* [1997] E.L.R. 214.

[15] *Ibid.*, p.218.

hearing as part of the investigation up to and including the opportunity to test the evidence of the complainant through cross-examination.

Firstly, the courts in Ireland have accepted, as a general principle, that an oral hearing with a facility of cross-examination is an important, although not automatic, element of natural and constitutional justice.

Secondly, those cases to the contrary often tend to be based on their own particular or unique facts and circumstances rather than on any general principles.

Cross-examinations and oral hearings are particularly important to many investigations of bullying and sexual harassment/harassment complaints since the effects on an employee's reputation are serious and there is invariably a conflict of evidence. In particular, it would be hard, in practice, to justify a procedure whereby the accused faced a meeting or interview, with or without representation, in which the evidence he submits would be subject to examination and scrutiny by an investigator whereas the same employee was never allowed the same opportunity to cross-examine and scrutinise the evidence of the complainant against him. Therefore, this is a matter upon which legal advice should always be sought on the particular circumstances of each case.

THE BIGGER THEY COME THE HARDER THEY FALL?

The rule of necessity

Having considered the scope of recommended anti-bullying/harassment procedure, the first question that a small business owner may ask is: *what if I don't have the numbers of personnel to implement such a procedure*?

It is a valid question. This is because the smaller an employer, the less opportunity and resources available, both human and financial, to find personnel that may be considered impartial within the business in order to adjudicate on complaints about employees. Indeed, in many small businesses, there may not be any middle managers/supervisors available at all to act as impartial adjudicators. There may only be the employer and his or her small workforce. Furthermore, in a small workplace, there is inevitably a high degree of proximity and closeness among the employees and between the employer and staff such that for someone within the business to adjudicate on any complaint may ordinarily be considered unfair or inappropriate.

In such an environment, it may be the case that an employee who makes a complaint of bullying/harassment and who does not wish to have the complaint dealt with informally (perhaps because of its seriousness) may believe that he or she will not get a fair hearing if a formal procedure is undertaken without an outside, independent person conducting it. This may be the case where an employee perceives that his employer may be biased in the situation.

This problem is recognised and the law applies what is called the '*rule of necessity*'. This rule has been confirmed by the Supreme Court, in the context of employment law, in recent years.[16] It simply means that, in certain circumstances, where the necessity of a situation may not allow for a completely independent party to investigate a claim, (as fair procedures would otherwise require) it will, nevertheless, be upheld as lawful. The courts recognise that, in any decision that an employer makes about the business, he is, by definition, never really a disinterested party. As such, to allow challenges to succeed on that basis alone would be to deprive employers from taking many necessary decisions in relation to their staff altogether. So long as an employer takes reasonably practicable steps in all the circumstances of his business to abide by all the other rules of fair procedures

---

[16] *Mooney v. An Post* [1998] E.L.R. 238.

outlined above, then the fact that there was no other option but to have an inquiry conducted by a person who may not be considered entirely at a remove from the dispute by one or other of the parties, is unlikely to invalidate the investigation on that ground alone.

For small businesses, in particular, this means that an employer, in the context of a small, close-knit workforce, who would otherwise be disqualified from conducting an inquiry under the rules against fair procedures, either because of a proximity to the parties or because of an absence of disinterest, can be held as competent and qualified to adjudicate *if no other duly qualified person or tribunal is available*.[17]

However, it must be remembered that this necessity rule is a very narrow exception to the general principle that fair procedures must be rigorously applied and an employer should attempt, if at all possible, to avoid being in that situation. Moreover, it does not negate the need to have an effective and fair anti-bullying/harassment policy and procedure in the first place. **It could not be relied upon where the intended adjudicator was connected in any way with the actual allegations at issue or was otherwise *actually* biased.**

The best way is to always try, where possible, to resolve a dispute, in these circumstances, informally or through mediation.

Agreed third party

One other possible way is the one recommended in the complaints procedures above. This now provides that, *where appropriate*, an agreed third party may conduct the formal procedure. There is no reason to suggest why this may not

---

[17] Smith, M, 'Workplace Bullying: Internal Investigations and Fair Procedures,' *Bar Review*, June/July 2002, p.272.

include an individual from outside the workforce. Therefore, an employer should carefully consider whether the request of an employee to bring in an independent party might be reasonable and appropriate in the circumstances of his case.

Small business at a disadvantage?

This is of much practical importance in bullying and harassment claims. The situation above sometimes puts smaller businesses at a disadvantage in defending claims. This is because the unavailability of a person in the business at a remove from a dispute may make it more tempting for disgruntled employees to deprive an employer of the opportunity to deal with a problem internally in the first instance. It allows small businesses a degree of protection against the claim that simply because they may not have a sufficiency of personnel at a remove from a dispute that this either taints *automatically* the procedure implemented or that it absolves an employee from invoking or complying with the anti-bullying/harassment procedure before bringing a constructive dismissal or compensation claim under the statutory or industrial relations mechanisms. However, employers should always act without delay in dealing with a complaint in these circumstances.

Larger employers, however, should *never* depart from their anti-bullying policies and procedures in any circumstances either by compromising on impartiality or by risking a potential conflict of interest. The larger an employer, the more human and financial resources available, and the less likely it is that the courts will entertain instances of bias in the course of investigations or disciplinary hearings affecting the rights and reputations of employees. This is acutely the role of HR management to ensure.[18]

---

[18] *Heneghan v. Western Regional Fisheries Board* [1986] I.L.R.M.

The role and legal obligations of HR best practice

In line with what has already been discussed in this chapter, an important consideration of HR best practice has also been recently articulated by the EAT in Ireland. The tribunal made the following conclusions.

The HR function in a company occupies a very special position between the employee and the employer. Accordingly, it owes a duty to those who repose confidence in it to take reasonable care and skill in the management of their affairs. All acts whereby the personnel function grossly departs from acceptable practices warrants the gravest of condemnation because this Department is entrusted with the safeguard of rights and entitlements protected by law. Both the management organisation and the employee structure look to the HR Department in relation to problems, disputes and difficulties. The objectives of Management, on the one hand, and the demands of the employees, on the other, may conflict. Therefore, the most important task of the HR function is to ensure a happy medium that will seek to resolve issues without interfering with the production of goods or services. As such, the principal role of HR is to advise the company and to formulate policies and strategies within the existing legal framework.

The HR function is bestowed as the ultimate receptor of complaints in relation to harassment, sexual harassment and bullying. This is so, primarily, because of and ensured by the detached existence of the unit within the management hierarchy and the confidential nature with which the unit approaches problems communicated to it. Accordingly, an over familiarity of this function with other management divisions should be guarded against in the interests of its

---

225; *O'Neill v. Beaumont Hospital Board* [1990] I.L.R.M. 419; *Charlton v. H.H. The Aga Khan's Stud Societe Civile* [1999] E.L.R. 136.

integrity, its independence and impartiality in dealing with issues of a personal and sensitive nature.[19]

Deciding to Suspend: What to be Aware and Wary of

Having received a complaint of bullying or harassment by an employee, an employer may have to decide, while not making any assumptions about the guilt or innocence of that accused employee, if it is appropriate to remove him or her from the workplace pending an investigation of the complaint. Similarly, if, having investigated the allegation, the complaint is ultimately upheld, the disciplinary procedure may be invoked and an employee may be suspended from the workplace for a period of time as a punishment.

This is an area that creates some of the greatest difficulties for employers, in practice, and one that frequently leads to court proceedings. Employers should always exercise extreme caution and should obtain legal advice on the circumstances of each individual case. This is particularly true of cases involving allegations of bullying, harassment or sexual harassment.

In Ireland, there are two recognised forms of suspension that must be distinguished from each other:

- A suspension as a holding operation pending further inquiries into a matter;
- A suspension as a disciplinary sanction.

Holding operation?

Where an employee is suspended as part of, or in the course of an investigation, into harassment, bullying or for a medical

[19] *Browne v. Ventelo Telecommunications (Irl) Limited* ,UD597/2001, July 16, 2002.

assessment arising from a risk of stress-related injury to a particular employee, then he is ordinarily **not** entitled to natural justice and fair procedures before being suspended. This is because there has not been any finding made against the employee at this stage.

Disciplinary sanction?

Where an employee is proposed for suspension from work as a form of punishment or penalty, then in that situation, the employee **is** entitled to natural justice and fair procedures before the decision to suspend is taken. Such a suspension has a serious implication for the reputation and livelihood of an employee. This distinction accords with both the general approach of the law and with common sense.[20]

To pay or not to pay?

Deductions from the wages of an employee are only permissible if:

- They are made under statute or any instrument made under statute;
- They are authorised to be made under a term of the contract of employment that must have been in force at the time of the deduction;
- The employee has given his advance written consent·[21]

---

[20] *Deegan & Ors v. The Minister for Finance* [2000] E.L.R. 190 *per* Keane C.J.; *Lewis v. Heffer* [1978] 3 All E.R. 354 *per* Denning M.R.

[21] Section 5 of the Payment of Wages Act 1991.

Disciplinary sanction

An employee suspended as a disciplinary sanction is ordinarily and lawfully deprived of his salary or wages entirely, or as a proportion thereof, throughout the duration of the suspension period.

However, it is very important that if an employer wishes to avail of this form of disciplinary sanction, it should be **expressly provided** for it as part of his contract of employment or as part of the anti-bullying or anti-harassment policies deemed to form part of the contract. An employer should confirm his authority to proceed in this manner before commencing disciplinary proceedings.

Holding operation

A suspension as a holding operation pending the outcome of investigations should always be on full pay and should not be open-ended. If there is no authority in the contract to deduct wages for this type of suspension, it *must* be on full pay.

A third category of suspension?

McNamara v. South Western Area Health Board: Killing two birds with the one stone?[22]

Background

This is a 2001 Irish case, in which the applicant, a consultant orthodontist with the respondent, was suspended pursuant to statute on suspicion that she had misconducted herself in relation to her office or was otherwise unfit to hold office. This suspension was effective *pending an inquiry* into the alleged misconduct or unfitness. However, this suspension

[22] [2001] E.L.R. 317. High Court *per* Kearns J.

had strong overtones of a disciplinary action, as it was without pay and open-ended in duration. Furthermore, the applicant had already been suspended by the Board on a previous occasion. The source of the dispute was the applicant's serious professional concerns and differences with the respondent regarding the safety of the orthodontic services provided by the Area Health Board. She brought a judicial review on the basis that she was denied fair procedures in the making of the decision to suspend her.

Judgment

The High Court decided that:

- Simply because the Board was entitled to do what it did under statute, this does not mean that it was not also obliged at every stage in the process, to discharge its duties in a fair, responsible and reasonable manner. As such, an allegation of misconduct against a senior consultant was a serious matter.
- The question of whether a suspension involves fair procedures hinges on:
    - The gravity of the reasons for the suspension;
    - The implications for the person concerned;
    - The likely adverse impacts for the employee following suspension.
- There could be decisions with adverse implications for a person affected but which nevertheless fall short of infringing their legal rights. It appears that these may rightly be considered as holding operations and do not necessarily attract a requirement of fair procedures.
- However, the situation here was in total contrast to such decisions. The suspensions were open-ended and non-specific in duration.

- *A suspension of a senior consultant without pay pending an inquiry into misconduct was more than a mere holding operation.*
- It was a sanction and a severe one at that which could only have had damaging implications for a *professional person* in the applicant's position. This was even more so where this was the second suspension which suggested that matters were moving towards the possible removal of the applicant altogether.
- The CEO of the respondent should, at least, have had some statement of the applicant's position on the matters in issue before suspending her. At the time of suspending, the CEO had not considered a detailed 13-page report furnished by the Applicant setting out her difficulties with the services.
- The suspension was intended to be a form of punishment, regardless of the legal forms observed, and that such punishment had been decided upon without fair procedures being carried out.

Consequences

On the basis of this recent High Court authority, for certain categories of professional or senior employees, at least, there may be a third way between holding and disciplinary suspensions. This is because a form of *suspension pending inquiry* may now arguably be more than a mere holding operation but, at the same time, not yet strictly a disciplinary sanction. When this will occur depends on the gravity of the allegations being inquired into, the seriousness of the consequences of the suspension for the employee, the duration of the suspension and whether it is without pay or at reduced pay. An interesting factor is that the Court was influenced by the analogy with the duties of a professional body charged with inquiring into the misconduct of a member of that profession. In such cases, it has been decided in Ireland that:

> "If a professional body is invested with the power of receiving complaints relating to a member of that profession and deciding *whether an inquiry should be put in motion*, the outcome of which might lead to the person complained *about being no longer able to practice his or her profession*, the body cannot be said to be exercising its power lawfully and fairly without the person complained about being informed of the complaint and the board having sight of any response to that complaint."[23]

This case was expressly referred to by the Court in *McNamara*. Therefore, in the appropriate case, it now seems that a suspension pending inquiry may *require* that fair procedures are provided to a certain type of professional employee subject to a serious charge of misconduct. However, since the facts of *McNamara* were particularly severe, in that the suspension was open-ended, without pay and was following on from an earlier one, further judicial decisions are needed before a definitive conclusion may be made on this point or on the scope of its application.

A note of caution: avoid the traps

However, in any investigation relating to bullying, harassment or sexual harassment, employers should now, at the very least, be wary of stumbling into any unnecessary traps. Therefore, even if there is authority to do so under statute or the contract of employment, the imposing of a suspension pending inquiry without pay increases a risk of being injuncted or judicially reviewed in court.

---

[23] *O'Ceallaigh v. An Bord Altranais* [2000] 4 I.R. 54.

Firstly, this is because the measure appears akin to a punishment or disciplinary sanction to which an employee should have been entitled to fair procedures before being suspended.

Secondly, the employee is being subjected to a penalty that, by definition, is being made before an actual finding or conclusion against him. This may, therefore, be deemed by a court or tribunal in any subsequent litigation to have the effect of tainting the overall investigation process. This is all the more so if the contract of employment also expressly provides for suspension without pay as a disciplinary sanction.[24]

Finally, depending on the gravity of the allegations, the professional status of an employee and the consequences for him or her, it may now be viewed as more than a mere holding operation and one that should have attracted fair procedures.

Therefore, an employer, whatever his authorisation, should avoid suspending an employee pending an investigation without pay *and* without fair procedures. This is all the more so in serious bullying and harassment cases, in cases involving senior or professional employees and where the suspension may be open-ended.

What to do in practice?

Inquiries

In most instances, an employee may be suspended on full pay pending the outcome and conclusion of the investigation into the matter. This should be for a defined period only. An employer may do this without the need to give the employee natural justice or fair procedures. Nevertheless, an employer should behave fairly, reasonably and responsibly along every

---

24 *Timmons v. Oglesby & Butler* [1999] E.L.R. 119.

step of the way. In other words, he or she must act with good faith.

In some instances, employers should also now bear in mind the risk that the graver the alleged wrongdoing and the more senior or professional the status of an employee, the greater the likelihood, on the basis of *McNamara*, that fair procedures are required. Where there is doubt, legal advice ought to be sought.

Discipline

However, once the investigation is completed and in the event that the employer has made a finding of wrongdoing on the part of the bullying or harassing employee, if the employer then proposes to suspend the employee for a period of time without pay as a punishment, the employee must be afforded fair procedures of the type discussed earlier.

In particular, the employee must be informed, at the very least, of the proposal to suspend him or her and must be given an opportunity both to make representations and to challenge the proposal. Where a right of appeal exists, the employee should also have the opportunity to use it in the event that the decision to suspend is made by management.

One final consideration on this area set to become a major bone of contention in the coming years involves the stress-related effects of the disciplinary hearings and procedures themselves (and indeed, the earlier investigative process) on the employees subject to them. In 2002, an interesting example of this phenomenon was reported and may be considered a shot across the bow of employers.

Manchester City Council v. Thurston. A case of damned if you do and damned if you don't?[25]

Background

This case focused on a practical problem faced by many employers. The Council in Manchester was concerned about the practice whereby employees who were due to face disciplinary proceedings take time off due to stress related illnesses. As such, the dispute involved the interpretation of a local government contractual sick pay scheme. This scheme provided that an employee whose absence on account of sickness was due or attributable to his own misconduct was not entitled to an allowance under the scheme except at the discretion of the employing authority. Mr Thurston, an electrician, was charged with misconduct, and, following a disciplinary hearing, was issued with a written warning for misbooking for work. Immediately after the imposition of this disciplinary sanction, he went off work ill. The medical officer of the employer found that he had anxiety or depression.

The employer took the view that this was a direct consequence of the misconduct of the employee and fell within the exclusion from sick pay under the scheme. As such, the employer thought it was entitled to withhold sick payments to him and did so.

Judgment

The EAT in England condemned this action on the following grounds.

1. The employee's absence was occasioned by a depressive illness that had begun some time prior to the disciplinary hearing and was not connected with his misconduct.

---

[25] [2002] I.R.L.R. 319 (May 5, 2002).

2. However, even if the employee's absence was due to the disciplinary sanction imposed upon him, the employer would still not be entitled to withhold sick pay because such an absence was not 'due or attributable to his own misconduct' within the meaning of the contractual term. The contractual term 'his own misconduct' should not be extended to include the consequences of that misconduct. Where there is a genuine psychiatric illness, even if a consequence of disciplinary proceedings that may be foreseeable to employees, it is still too remote to come within the construction of a punitive contractual term such as here.
3. In any event, the employer should have exercised its contractual discretion to make payments in favour of the employee, having regard to the nature of the incident for which he was disciplined and also the fact that he was clearly suffering from depression. The employers also failed to produce evidence to show the consistency and extent of this policy to withhold sick pay.

Lessons?

An employee on sick leave for psychiatric ill health must be treated exactly in the same way provided for in the contract as any other employee entitled to such leave even if that employee now has a disciplinary sanction hanging over him. An employee need not have suffered from or been diagnosed with such an illness at any time prior to being disciplined but the illness can be as a result of the discipline process itself.

The employee on leave with a validly diagnosed psychiatric illness cannot be penalised indirectly through the withholding of his/her contractual sick pay for the same misconduct for which he/she has been already been sanctioned. Where the contract provides otherwise, this is now unlawful in England.

On all occasions, psychiatric illness, as a general principle, must be dealt with separately from any instances of misconduct that an employee may also be engaged in. Furthermore, if prior to an investigation of a complaint, the bullying or harassment was medically diagnosed as having being caused by a psychiatric illness, under this decision it might now be the case that the individual cannot be punished at all since an employer may be deemed to be penalising his illness rather than the misconduct it created.

Conclusions: A Brave New World?

Therefore, the coming years will be ones of increasing change and transformation for the importance accorded to the eradication of work-related stress, bullying and harassment in the course of employment. In turn, this will also have a significant impact on the duties and obligations expected of employers in promoting this effort. Indeed, these efforts will have an impact on the way things are done in the traditional workplace that are likely to be completely unrelated to simple concerns about work-related stress itself. There is a growing awareness among employees and the general public of these problems and this will be reflected in a greater number of claims before the courts and tribunals of this country over the coming years. The failure of businesses, of all types, to meet their obligations, therefore, now results in a significantly greater exposure to liability on a variety of differing grounds. The most serious exposure lurks ever-present in the realm of civil damages and monetary compensation. In order to avoid the day when this may befall his or her business, an employer must firstly now adopt policies and procedures incorporating the latest recommended practices or, where they are already present, keep them under ongoing review and updated. In light of new and ever-increasing legal and health and safety developments, this is of particular importance. In relation to a second thing employers should do, it is simply this: be vigilant, be fair and always, always **Apply and Stick to Your Procedures!**

Index